Praise for *Learning* .

"Paul's excellent new book includes great practical tips and challenges long established processes to ensure that learning leads to improved performance. *Learning Transfer at Work* is a must read for all L&D professionals."

Daniel Rowlinson
Learning and Development Manager, Searcys

"Paul has shone a light on an often ignored but critical aspect of learning. This isn't just a dry academic analysis; he has gathered case studies and has again produced an extensive list of pragmatic actions."

Jim Potts PFHEA
Deputy Head Training and Education, Defence Academy of the UK

"Paul addresses this particular elephant in the room head on. Learning transfer may not be the sexiest of topics in the learning and development sector but it is one of the most critical, and Paul skilfully combines research, theory and practitioner views. Any L&D professional's practice will be enhanced by this book."

Mike Shaw
Senior Learning & Development Professional

"This book calls out the elephant in many L&D rooms; if we don't ensure a positive impact from development activities on organisational goals, we are wasting valuable time and resources. Paul highlights the importance of systemic thinking. Learning transfer is not solely dependent on whether an initiative in itself is good, but involves the vital questions around whether needs are accurately defined, who the learning is aimed at and how well the learners are prepared and supported once back in their workplace."

Andy Lancaster
Head of L&D, Chartered Institute of Personnel and Development (CIPD)

"Learning transfer has been L&D's dirty little secret for too long. Too much of what learning teams do is well intentioned but ultimately underwhelming. Paul Matthews' excellent book is packed with actionable hints, tips and strategies which will enhance the work of anyone who is serious about ensuring that learning interventions make a positive difference to employee's skills and an organisation's capability."

Robin Hoyle, Writer
Head of Learning Innovation at Huthwaite International
Chair of the World of Learning Conference

Anyone who is looking to the future of learning must read this book. It asks questions which we assume L&D people already have the answers to, and frames the answers from other perspectives. Enlightening!

Nathan Baker
Director of Engineering Knowledge, Institution of Civil Engineers

"Learning transfer is actually the most critical piece of the learning puzzle, without it the entire exercise is wasted. Learning Transfer at Work finally offers some answers on how to pin this down and really make it happen, a great read!"

Joe Tidman
Head of Learning and Development, Johnson Matthey

"In this book, Paul takes one of the most difficult subjects for Learning and Development and deals with it in a no-nonsense style that will constantly challenge everyone who reads it. We have to know that we are truly making a difference for people AND the businesses they work for. The book is full of the latest insights, practical tips and ideas as well as traditional concepts with new twists. This will be a 'must read' and 'need to put into practice' for everyone in my team."

Jeff Uden
Head of Talent, Iceland Foods

Learning Transfer
AT WORK

To Con + Bob

Thanks!

Paul.

PAUL MATTHEWS

Learning Transfer
AT WORK

HOW TO ENSURE TRAINING >> PERFORMANCE

Three Faces Publishing

Learning Transfer at Work
How to ensure training >> Performance

Copyright © Paul Matthews 2018

The right of Paul Matthews to be identified as the author of this work has been asserted by him in accordance with the Copyright, Designs and Patents Act, 1988.

First published in 2018 by
Three Faces Publishing
Alchemy House
17 Faraday Drive
Milton Keynes
MK5 7DD
United Kingdom

www.threefacespublishing.com
info@threefacespublishing.com

British Library Cataloguing in Publication Data
A CIP catalogue record for this book is available from the British Library

Paperback ISBN: 978-1-909552-06-7
Kindle ISBN: 978-1-909552-07-4

The publisher's policy is to use paper manufactured from sustainable forests.

Printed and bound in the UK by TJ International Ltd, Padstow, Cornwall

Typeset by Ramesh Kumar Pitchai

Thank you

We rarely travel alone.

Many people have been involved with bringing this book into being; from people who were prepared to indulge me in endless conversations about the core ideas, to people like Diana Lodge and Anita Vermaak who had a much more hands-on role in converting the ideas into a workable manuscript, and many others who encouraged me. In particular I would like to thank the people who have sent in the contributions you will see later in the book. These add a richness of thought I could never have achieved on my own.

To one and all... a heartfelt thanks for helping me on my journey.

Paul

Contents

Foreword

I meet many inspirational learning professionals in my role as Head of Learning and Development at the Chartered Institute of Personnel and Development (CIPD). And, as part of that global learning network, I count Paul Matthews as a key figure who understands what it takes to deliver effective learning in organisations.

His previous books *"Informal Learning at Work: How to Boost Performance in Tough Times"* and *"Capability at Work: How to Solve the Performance Puzzle"* establish the DNA of his thought-leadership; an astute diagnosis of the challenges faced by learning practitioners and highly pragmatic solutions that help organisations shift in performance and productivity. At CIPD we know that transformative L&D practice is principles-led, evidence-based and outcomes-driven, Paul ticks all those boxes!

I was therefore delighted to be asked by Paul to write the foreword for this latest book *"Learning Transfer at Work: How to Ensure Training >> Performance"* knowing full well that it would bring a necessary challenge.

The theme of learning transfer must be of the highest priority to all those involved with organisational learning. The investment in learning can be significant and there must be an expectation that the outlay will drive impact. In our increasingly competitive and fast-changing world results matter, and development must have a clear link to measurable outcomes.

This book calls out the elephant in many L&D rooms; if we don't ensure a positive impact from development activities on organisational goals, we are wasting valuable time and resources. Paul highlights the importance of systemic thinking. Learning transfer is not solely dependent on whether an initiative in itself is good, but involves the vital questions around whether needs are accurately defined, who the learning is aimed at and how well the learners are prepared and supported once back in their workplace.

Sadly, L&D practitioners often ignore these components and perpetuate a culture in which there is a lack of accountability for learning transfer. The book highlights that for impact to be a reality, learning professionals must be thoughtful and objective in their assessment of learning but also in providing support to all involved in the learning ecosystem. Every stakeholder in a development scenario must play their part and commit to ensuring effective transfer takes place.

This requires a shift in mindset, which in itself is no mean feat, and the willingness to embrace rigorous and creative approaches.

In addition, the chapter on L&D brand poses demanding questions of learning teams as to how they and the organisation view the learning and development offering. The answer is often, sadly, not encouraging and improving perceptions is inextricably linked to demonstrating impact.

As with all Paul's books, having painted a clear picture of the challenge, he provides strategies to drive improvements in learning transfer including the insightful research work of Dr Weinbauer-Heidel who has defined '12 Levers of Transfer Effectiveness'. Together these books and their practical ingredients create a recipe to increase learning transfer and impact.

So, I commend the book to you, it's a thought-provoking read! But more than that, I implore all of us that play a part in organisational learning to act on the principles. I am reminded of a quote by the great Leonardo da Vinci: *"I have been impressed with the urgency of doing. Knowing is not enough. We must apply. Being willing is not enough. We must do."*

Now is the time to take the steps needed to make learning transfer the reality … and the norm!

Andy Lancaster
Head of L&D, Chartered Institute of Personnel and Development (CIPD)
Twitter: @AndyLancasterUK

Introduction

Well, first it was going to be another of my Best Practice Guides, but it got too big for that.

Then it was going to be an eBook, but it kept growing. It is a big subject.

So I bowed to the inevitable and started the journey to writing another book. Yes, I know; I said that two L&D books were enough, but this new one on Learning Transfer is important!

Learning transfer is the elephant in many rooms I have been in where a training programme is under discussion. When I point at the elephant, there is usually an acknowledgement of its existence, followed by a slide back into the comforting rut of course delivery.

Yet to me, this elephant is BIG, and impossible to ignore. In reality, the case for proactively driving the learning transfer process is self-evident, but so many people choose to behave as if the elephant is not there. Why?

Ignoring this elephant is expensive. Besides, it really annoys the elephant!

This book is full of ideas; practical ideas you can use to do two things...
1. Convince those around you that the learning transfer elephant is real
2. Introduce processes and activities that deal with this elephant.

I have attempted to include...
   • Why learning transfer is the elephant in the room

- A convincing argument that you MUST practise proactive learning transfer
- Helpful information so you can convince others of its necessity
- The mindset required for learning transfer
- Where and when to start planning learning transfer
- Common pitfalls and barriers to getting it right
- Common myths and misunderstandings
- Lots of tools and practical ideas to help you be successful.

I hope you find it helpful :-)

Paul Matthews
August 30th, 2018

PS This quote from George Orwell sums up why I didn't want to write another book.

"Writing a book is a horrible, exhausting struggle, like a long bout of some painful illness. One would never undertake such a thing if one were not driven on by some demon whom one can neither resist nor understand."

Part 1: Overview

What is learning transfer?

"Begin at the beginning," the King said, very gravely, "and go on till you come to the end: then stop."

Lewis Carroll, Alice in Wonderland

Despite this sage advice from the King of Hearts, most training fails because it does not start at the beginning and does not keep going until the end. The Queen of Hearts would probably shout, "Off with their heads!" for such a transgression, so it is lucky that we are not L&D practitioners in Wonderland. Nevertheless, to avoid even the possibility of beheading, let's begin at our beginning and define what we mean by 'learning transfer'. Then we can proceed to explore the true beginning of training, and when it has reached the end.

Like many terms, the phrase 'learning transfer' seems to mean different things to different people. In organisational learning, it usually refers to the implementation of learning that has happened in a prior formal event, such as a training course or an e-learning course. Every definition I have seen talks about the application of learning, so the term learning transfer means much more than just transfer, or movement, of learning from one place to another.

It also means the translation and application of the learnt knowledge, skills and attitudes into effective action that improves job performance, is sustained over time and is beneficial for the output of the workflow.

The goal of training is to make the learning gained from the training experience portable, so that the learner takes it to new places where it can be used. If the training programme does not achieve significant transfer, and subsequent deployment of the learning, it's not worth much! Learning transfer underpins the whole notion of training, and yet too often we focus on the transmission of information from the trainer to the trainee, and then the retention of the information by the trainee. We tend to overlook the primary purpose of organisational training: an improved employee performance that can only happen when there is sufficient learning transfer. A huge amount of money is spent annually on employee training, yet past studies have shown that failure of transfer from the training setting to the real job is common.

Not surprisingly, employers are increasingly demanding that training yields a measurable and meaningful return on their investment. Hopefully, L&D trainers are finally waking up to the fact that organisations are going to start holding them more accountable and therefore they must influence beyond the training room. Keeping themselves inside the boundaries of training and other formal interventions does not generate results that are comfortable to report in those accountability conversations. Indeed, the reputation of L&D is not encouraging, as surveys show that most business leaders doubt the efficacy of L&D. A Deloitte[1] study stated that 84% of CEOs believe that L&D is an important component in the pursuit of talent and leadership, but only 39% agree that L&D is ready.

A McKinsey study (May, 2016)[2] stated that "Only 57% of the respondents believe that their academies are 'very or fully aligned' with corporate priorities. Even fewer (52%) reported that these institutions enable their companies to meet strategic objectives." These sentiments at senior management levels mean that there is an emerging trend where demonstrating business impact will become vital to securing L&D budget. Most organisations have already faced significant reductions in L&D budget during the recent tougher economic times, and now there is increasing scrutiny surrounding the budget that is still being spent.

[1] Deloitte, *Reinventing HR*, 2015. http://dupress.com/articles/reinventing-hr-human-resources-humancapital-trends-2015

[2] McKinsey Quarterly, *Learning at the speed of business* (May, 2016)

Rather than being based on evidence, most investment in training and development appears to be based on faith that it will work or because it is regarded as a 'given good', but that faith seems to be misplaced. All too often the way we try to achieve learning is based on flawed models built around one big event. Information and skills from events that only cover concepts once have been shown to yield little long-term retention, even when quality and satisfaction ratings for the learning event are high. One researcher (Goldstein, 1986)[3] has suggested that 90% of all training is a waste of time and money – people either knew it already, forgot it quickly or simply didn't need it/couldn't use it in their jobs. That is an old study, but consider this statement from a Saratoga/PWC report (2005)[4], "Organisations across Europe spent £1.03 billion on leadership training in 2003 with little evidence of a major return." More recently, in an ATD article (August 2017)[5] Tris Brown wrote, "LSA Global has measured more than 800 training projects; and we have found that training alone, even when it is highly customized and targeted, only changes the on-the-job behavior and performance of one in five participants on average." It seems like things have not changed much over the years.

My hope is that in sharing this information about learning transfer, the argument to include effective transfer strategies will prove so compelling and obvious that you will no longer be able to imagine delivering any training without them. In fact, it should become obvious that not using transfer strategies when you could would be tantamount to malpractice for any learning and development professional. (It's a crime, if not quite deserving the capital punishment the Queen of Hearts was so fond of dishing out.)

Of course, we are not just talking about wasted training budget here. Every day an employee isn't ready to work and ready to be independently productive carries a cost, not a profit. Shortening the 'speed to skill' time saves money as well as reducing frustration, improving morale and providing other side benefits, such as lower attrition rates. If shrinking the time to proficiency is one of the most significant contributions that L&D can make to an organisation, learning transfer is the key to achieving this.

---

[3] I.L. Goldstein, *Training in Organisations: Needs Assessment, Development and Evaluation*, 1986

[4] Saratoga/PWC *Key Trends in Human Capital* report, 2005

[5] ATD article 'How Can You Ensure Transfer of Training to Get the Results Business Leaders Want' (August 2017) Tris Brown

We should be aware that the term 'learning transfer' can have other meanings. For example, in the education sector, it usually means the transfer of 'learning' from teacher to student, so perhaps a better term in education would be 'knowledge acquisition'. This acquisition of knowledge lends itself to being examined later for its retention, and in education, exam results are a measure of success. This book, however, is about learning transfer where the focus is on specific improvements in employee performance and results, rather than solely on what has been learned and its retention. We are talking about a shift in focus from what it takes to complete a training event to what it takes to get employees proficient at their job using the material from the training event.

Learning transfer is about change resulting from a process that takes place to a lesser or greater degree following a formal learning intervention. The degree to which it occurs has a direct impact on the value the organisation will harvest from this investment. Successful learning transfer depends on a mindset that permeates the entire learning programme, from design through delivery to the end game. It depends on a focus on business benefits rather than learning outcomes.

In this practical book, I will focus on training as the formal learning intervention, so I have used the term 'trainee', though it could have been 'delegate' or 'learner'. There is always debate about semantics, and which word we 'should' be using. Some would also argue that there is a difference between training transfer and learning transfer on the basis that training and learning are two different things. Given that learning is one of the goals of training, I find it rather difficult to separate the two. There are better things to spend our time on than arguing over which words to use, but I would suggest that it is a good idea to settle on the term that you use within your own organisation and keep it consistent.

Despite the book's focus on training, the same learning transfer ideas and processes could be applied to anything else you might consider 'formal learning', or that would fall into the '10' of the 70:20:10 learning model. For those not yet aware of this model and its recent popularity as a 'compass' for L&D strategy, the 70:20:10 model posits that
- around 70% of learning comes from experience, experiment and reflection
- around 20% derives from working with others
- around 10% comes from planned learning solutions

For more on this model and how to utilise the principles that arise from it, I recommend the work of Charles Jennings and his colleagues at the 70:20:10 Institute at https://702010institute.com.

It has been said that to avoid learning transfer problems, don't do any training. Instead do other things that bring learning and provide tasks that embed behaviour change directly into the workflow. However, training is unlikely to disappear any time soon. It is still the mainstay intervention of most learning and development departments. According to the Towards Maturity benchmark report *Unlocking Potential* (November, 2016), 56% of learning provision is delivered face-to-face and the use of technology in learning is focused on online course delivery rather than performance support. There is considerable pressure to reduce the amount of face-to-face training because it is seen as too costly in comparison to online training, but I maintain that it has its place. The importance of this physical separation from the daily grind should not be underestimated. If employees have no opportunity to step away from their working environments, the same old behaviour, for good and ill, is constantly reinforced, and the chance for more reflective, committed learning is lost. Harvard professor Ronald Heifetz calls this a 'balcony moment': the imperative for leaders to leave the dance floor periodically and reflect on the patterns and movement below.

It's interesting that people are seeking to reduce training, rather than fix the major issue with it: lack of learning transfer. Is this quest to reduce traditional training time a result of disillusionment with training as a tool? Is it because people feel there must be something better? Or is it simply a way to reduce costs? If we get learning transfer right, training and other formal interventions are viable tools to use in the quest to improve organisational performance. This in no way means that all training currently taking place should keep running and just have some learning transfer bolted onto it. There is more to it than simply moving towards a closer relationship between learning and work. As organisations attain higher levels of learning maturity, their mindset about employee development shifts away from viewing learning and development as stand-alone, separate, external activities. Instead they view learning and work as intimately connected, and development happening as part of their employees' day-to-day work. Mature learning organisations are increasingly discarding long-held or traditional beliefs about how learning should be created and facilitated, and are instead focusing on creating the right conditions, context and culture for learning to take place. Peter Senge, who wrote the seminal book, *The Fifth Discipline: The Art and Practice of learning in Organisations,* said in an interview, "A learning organisation is a group of people working together collectively to enhance their capabilities to create results they really care about."

This cultural shift is surely vital, because learning transfer following a formal event is a process that is in turn part of a much longer process that predates the event, and extends long after it, all of which plays out within the cultural environment. The whole longer process and its surroundings must be considered if you want the learning transfer component to be successful. As with a chain, the entire process is only as strong as its weakest link. We therefore need to look at all the links in this chain, including those parts of the process that predate the actual learning transfer, because these set up the initial conditions and inputs. And since the entire process takes place over time, you can think of it as a workflow.

It is advantageous to think of learning transfer taking place as the result of a workflow. The term 'workflow' presupposes a sequence of tasks, or even mini-workflows, that build on each other, step by step, over a period of time. It is an orchestrated and repeatable pattern of activities that takes specified inputs and, all going well, culminates in a specified set of outputs. The word 'workflow' reminds us of the fact that people must DO something rather than intellectually learn something. Albert Einstein said "Learning is an experience. Everything else is just information". So think of the formal training event as simply one step in the experiential workflow that is required to get the results you want. A traditional training course, without an effective learning transfer workflow wrapped around it, is most unlikely to deliver employee behaviour change or any significant business benefits. Without further intervention, the traditional structured and linear nature of learning in the classroom does not prepare people well for the more complex and ambiguous world of work.

As with any workflow, if the inputs are inadequate, the learning transfer part of the workflow can never produce the desired results. This of course highlights the need to measure the inputs and outputs to ensure they are adequate. Measure the inputs in two categories: those required at the nominal beginning of the workflow, and those required to support each step of the workflow that feeds into the next. Measure the final outputs to ensure that you are getting the necessary returns for the process to be worth doing at all. These final measures should relate to existing business performance measures and can also be based on tools and concepts introduced by Dr Donald Kirkpatrick, Dr Jack Phillips, Prof. Robert O Brinkerhoff and others that measure learning success.

So as with any other business workflow, learning transfer is part of a larger system, part of an even longer chain of interrelated workflows, and should always be considered within the context of the larger system. Unfortunately, learning transfer itself is a very weak link in most organisational systems. "For the most part, learning does not lead to better organisational performance, because people soon revert to their old ways of doing things", according to 'Why Leadership Training Fails – and What to Do About It', an article in the *Harvard Business Review* (October, 2016). In their paper "*Training Transfer: An Integrative Literature Review*" (2007) Burke and Hitchens state "Estimates of the exact extent of the transfer problem vary, ... to Saks' (2002) survey data, which suggest about 40% of trainees fail to transfer immediately after training, 70% falter in transfer one year after the program, and ultimately only 50% of training investments result in organizational or individual improvements. Given these estimates, it is clear that learning investments continue to yield deficient results..." What they are saying is that returning trainees had less power to change the system surrounding them than the power the system had to maintain its inertia and shape them. Trainees tend to revert/conform to the system after doing training. However, it is possible to empower the trainees and to shift the culture in the system so it becomes fertile ground for growth and development.

Despite the common-sense argument that training that is not used is wasted money, the tools and activities to ensure successful learning transfer are often not used at all, or they are only used superficially and thus have little impact. This is not to say that all training is wasted. There are certainly training programmes that are successful in achieving the desired business results, but these are in the minority when compared to the vast amount of training that is delivered each year.

In many cases, if the system does not change, it is unlikely to support individual change, and may well be inimical to it. There are considerable bodies of research that show that the effect of training over the longer term is limited, and yet senior teams still see it as the solution. One reason for this is that they view their organisation as an aggregation of individuals. Therefore, people must be selected for and trained with the right knowledge and skills to execute their strategy and improve the organisation's performance. Competency frameworks are developed to suit the organisational strategy, and training courses follow.

This makes very little, if any, allowance for the fact that organisations are systems of interacting elements, with structures and processes and leadership styles, as well as professional and cultural backgrounds.

If we see the organisation as a system with many interacting components, and the captain of the ship/system is the senior team, it can be difficult to confront that senior team with an uncomfortable truth: failure to execute on strategy and change organisational behaviour is not down to individual worker deficiencies but is due to the way that the captain is steering the ship. It is much easier for the captain to hear that members of the crew need training than it is for him to hear that his own performance is contributing to the problem.

Thankfully, although a major factor in learning transfer, the culture of the organisation is not the only determinant. There are many others, which in turn would be more powerful when wielded within a supportive culture. Michael Leimbach of Wilson Learning conducted a study to show the impact of learning transfer activities. He wrote an article for *TrainingZone* in July 2013 based on the results of his research, covering 32 research studies from recent years that compared the impact of training workshops alone with training workshops plus one or more learning transfer activities. He states, "This research allowed us to identify 11 specific actions that have a significant impact on whether training results in measurable performance improvement. Overall, we found that if an organisation implemented all these actions, they could improve the effectiveness of their learning by over 180%." Learning transfer is a game we can win.

In general, the research clearly shows that the amount of learning that is transferred back to the job doesn't solely depend on how good the training course was. It also depends on
- The importance given to learning and development by the organisation and whether the right training need was identified for the right person in the right job
- How well the training course was designed to meet that need and how well the learners were prepared for the learning experience
- How well the trainers understood the learners' needs and how best to help them learn
- To what extent the learner was supported while trying to use the learning back at work.

Why do we avoid it?

Never ignore the elephant in the room. That's rude; play with it and introduce it.

Donna Lynn Hope

As was pointed out in the introduction to this book, learning transfer seems to be the resident elephant in many rooms where a training programme is under discussion. When I point at the elephant, there is usually an acknowledgement of its existence, followed by a slide back into the comforting rut of course delivery. "Yeah, we need to do something about that, but right now we need to focus on the logistics for all the trainees from the EMEA region." Perhaps the elephant has been there for so long that people in L&D now just assume that it's part of the furniture.

To me, this elephant is BIG, and impossible to ignore. In fact, the learning transfer elephant, because of the wasted money it represents, is even bigger than the other two elephants that lurk in the room as well. (We will meet these companion elephants later, because they are peripheral to learning transfer but also have an impact.)

To me, the case for proactively driving the learning transfer process is self-evident, and yet so many people choose to behave as if the elephant doesn't exist. Why? If we look at some of the reasons, we can start to understand how to change the conversation. By the way, some of what follows may annoy you as I am being a bit provocative, or you may find you are gritting your teeth and wishing you didn't agree.

1. I never really thought about it. "Elephant? Really? Where? No-one else is mentioning it."

Actually, many people are talking about the elephant in books, on blogs, at conferences. This is nothing new, and not uncommon. They may not call it 'learning transfer'. They may use terms like 'making learning stick', 'making training effective', 'embedding learning' and many others. Now that you are aware, start to notice how often you hear talk of the elephant. If your colleagues don't talk about the elephant, you will need to look outside your own organisation to avoid the internal groupthink that is ignoring the elephant. Then come back and ask some pointed questions about training effectiveness within your own organisation and what might need to be done to make training more effective. Why do so many people in L&D do little or nothing about learning transfer when doing something is such simple common sense?

2. L&D say their job is to train people or deliver other formal learning. "You asked for training; you got it. Job done. Our responsibility finishes at the end of the course. Learning transfer is not our responsibility." In effect, they are saying that their job is delivering information and not building skills that require practice based on that information. They see the necessary skill building and behaviour change as a job for those out in the field.

This attitude arises when L&D set themselves up as an order taker, as a shopkeeper. One of the common tools that contribute to this paradigm is the traditional Learning Management System (LMS), with its list of courses and events that people can book to attend. It's like ordering something off an online shopping site where the seller is not involved in any way with how the product will be used. Some even have an algorithm that says, "Other learners who attended this course also attended these other courses."

A common lament I hear among L&D people is their lack of access to the top table and exclusion from top-level decision making. I often find that the people with this lament are the very same people who have the 'shopkeeper attitude'. Think about it for a minute. Would you, as a senior decision maker in an organisation, want to have the head shopkeeper from a small peripheral department at your board table? Not likely.

So, start getting interested in how people are using your training courses, and why they order them in the first place. Assume that at least part of the process of learning transfer is your responsibility and notice how that shifts your thinking about your role as a trainer and as a course/ programme designer. People want a training course to solve a problem they have. What is that problem? Become someone who solves problems for people rather than someone who just sells stuff that might be a solution if the buyer has chosen wisely. If we are buying anything other than a commodity, we really appreciate the expertise of a salesperson who takes the time and effort to find out what problem we are trying to solve and then guides us to a viable solution.

3. L&D has outsourced the training, and the external training provider is primarily interested in selling training.

   If the subject of learning transfer is even discussed, it becomes a finger pointing exercise. The training company says that it is up to the client to handle learning transfer activities, and the client points at the training company saying that their training course has not worked.

   To me, responsibility lies in both camps. The procurement process within the client company should be making sure that it is buying all the components needed to ensure the success of the training course. Otherwise, it is a bit like buying a car without the wheels. Equally, the selling process within the training provider should ensure that their client understands the need for effective learning transfer and should provide help and support to put that in place.

   Unfortunately, it seems to be acceptable to buy training, and to sell training, without wheels.

4. Management says it's not their responsibility. They say that their job is operational excellence, not staff development. "L&D should be doing staff development."

   There are two aspects to this. One is that most management role job descriptions include a section that states their responsibility for developing the members of their team. If the job description does not include this responsibility, it should. The second aspect, which they also cannot run away from, is that most of the learning that happens at work, happens on their watch in the general day-to-day workflow. The 70:20:10 learning model tells us this, and even a moment's reflection also tells us this from our own experience of where we learned to do what we do at work.

What most managers don't understand is that, unbeknownst to them, they have superpowers. These powers manifest themselves every time the manager answers a question, delegates a task, or has a conversation or other form of interaction with a team member. They also manifest when a team member observes how their manager interacts with anybody else – either directly or in any other way. By their actions, the manager sets the mini-culture within the team to be accountable or not, to learn or not, to blame or not, to help or not, to experiment or not, to seek excellence or not, to serve customers or not, to go the extra mile or not. Employees look to their manager for a lead to understand what is rewarded and what is frowned upon.

Every manager has an immense effect on how their team functions and performs, and most don't begin to comprehend the magnitude of their power. They are 'developing' their team members to behave a certain way by being the manager they are, and they have far more power over developing/moulding team behaviour than L&D ever will. A manager cannot abdicate their input into staff development because it is already baked into their role. They have no choice in the matter. The question is whether they will become aware of their power and use it consciously, or whether they remain unaware and use it haphazardly.

5. Some would say that if we mandate that learning transfer is a management responsibility, managers couldn't do it effectively anyway because they don't have the time/skill/inclination/support. "Our managers are not trained coaches."

This excuse is really scary because of the aforementioned superpowers. If people are unaware of their superpowers, the best we can hope for is that the use of those powers for better or for worse cancels out into some overall neutral effect. But think how much is to be gained by harnessing them for the greater good.

We need to take a leaf from the superhero comic books where the nascent hero becomes aware of their powers and then ideally learns from a teacher to use them wisely. In comic land, a superhero who uses their powers for the greater good is one of the good guys, and one who gets seduced into using their powers for their own gains, or just doesn't care about the consequences of their actions, is one of the bad guys.

Good managers should already have an amount of time in their schedules for regular, maybe weekly, one-on-ones, and discussions about learning transfer from a recent training course can take place in that time. But many managers don't do this, and therefore have no protected time available for learning transfer support. To me, a manager who admits to not doing one-on-ones is admitting to being a poor manager of their team, a poor manager of their time, and a poor manager of their boss who has given them their workload, which they have accepted.

Programmes followed by one-on-one coaching show a better transfer of learning. Olivero, Bane and Kopelman[6] conducted a study involving 31 managers from a public agency who took part in a conventional managerial training programme. This was followed by eight weeks of one-on-one executive coaching. Analysis revealed that the training alone increased manager productivity by 22.4%, while coaching, which involved goal setting, problem solving, practice, feedback, supervisory involvement, evaluation, and public presentation, increased manager productivity by 88%. Professional coaching for learning transfer works. This is to be expected, given that coaching is a tool used to help people attain their goals.

It is true that a manager cannot be expected to have the same level of coaching and mentoring skills as a trained coach and therefore may not be able to support their team member in the same way as a professional. However, the manager is usually present from day to day, where an external coach is not. The manager has an enormous impact because of their own attitude towards learning and experimenting with new ideas, and because of the way they manage the environment around the trainee as they embed their new learning. The manager can also be supported

---

[6] Published in *Public Personnel Management* (Vol 26, 1997), 'Executive coaching as a transfer of training tool'.

with tips and guides on how to provide support for team members who are doing a training course. They could even be supported by coaches if the programme warrants it.

In my opinion, letting managers off the hook for supporting learning transfer, which is something that is largely within their sphere of influence and responsibility, is just perpetuating an unacceptable situation from generation to generation of managers. Stop the cycle and get the managers involved as coaches – no matter what it costs. Later in the book there are practical ideas to help you do this.

Plus, the rewards for moving towards a coaching culture are significant. According to a Bersin by Deloitte[7] research study, organizations that are highly effective at coaching were approximately 30% more likely to have strong business results and 33% more effective at engaging employees. They also enjoyed 42% higher employee productivity and were rated 75% higher in hiring the best people, developing employees and retaining their top people.

6. Doing things to facilitate the learning transfer process takes time, money and resources that we do not have. "Basically, we can't afford to do it."

If you can't afford to do effective learning transfer, it seems rather silly to waste money on training that will, as a result, be largely ineffective. Think of it this way. You have a budget for L&D. Consider how you can get the most business benefit from that budget rather than how you can deliver the most trainings. And note that focusing on business benefits, performance, productivity and results may win you larger budgets.

7. "Our people are not ready for that kind of change." Whenever I hear this excuse, in my mind I am thinking, 'This L&D person is not ready to fight for that kind of change.'

The next thing that goes through my mind is 'What are they scared will be uncovered by asking people to do something with what they

---

7 *High-Impact Performance Management: Maximizing Performance Coaching*, Stacia Sherman Garr, Bersin by Deloitte. (www.bersin.com/News/Details. aspx?id=15040)

have learned on a training course, and asking other people, such as their managers, to help them?' Sure, people, especially managers, will need support, but to say baldly that managers are not ready, therefore introducing learning transfer is not possible?

8. "We know we should be doing something about learning transfer, but we don't know how to modify our training programmes to include it."

Keep reading, you are in the right place. Look for other resources on the web and other books, such as those in a short list of companion reading in the Appendix.

9. "We do some stuff on learning transfer and it doesn't seem to make any real difference."

Most training courses do indeed have things tagged on that are designed to encourage learning transfer. This might be something as simple as asking trainees to set some goals related to the course or asking the line manager to have a conversation with the trainee about the course. The problem is that not enough is done, and often what is done, like the two examples mentioned, are largely ineffective for reasons we will explore later. To deliver effective learning transfer, you need to commit to the process and develop a full workflow that has all the elements needed to get the results you want. Keep reading.

10. "We have never done it before, and no one is asking for it, so why change things?"

People may not be asking for learning transfer by name because they don't know what they don't know, but they are probably asking for better training because they want better results from training. Or they are asking for cheaper and quicker training so the results they are accustomed to getting don't seem so expensive. Is there pressure on your L&D budget because it is seen as an organisational spend that does not produce the results that could be gained by spending that money elsewhere in the organisation? Have you ever mentioned the fact that you could wrap a workflow/programme around a training course to improve the results it gets?

Those who ask for training do so often on this assumption…
Training = exposure to content
Content exposure = learning
Learning = behaviour change
Behaviour change = better performance and results.
In other words, they erroneously believe that L&D has sacks full of pixie dust in the back room to sprinkle on trainees, which means that trainees return from a training course with their new knowledge and skills fully operational. Of course, if you do have any pixie dust left, you don't need to do anything about learning transfer and you can give this book to someone who doesn't know where to buy pixie dust.

11. "Our history shows that training doesn't have much impact anyway, so why add more cost to the process".

This excuse obviously begs the question as to why they are doing the training in the first place. It's analogous to a man standing in front of a fireplace with an armful of wood insisting that the fire gives him more heat before he gives it more wood.

12. This training is only for compliance purposes because we need to tick some regulatory boxes. "Getting the trainees through the test is all that matters."

I can understand this at the surface level, but to me, this seems a short-term approach. If there are regulations in place to drive/control how people behave in certain regulated circumstances, one would hope that organisations try and achieve those behaviours. We are therefore back to the same need for effective learning transfer that achieves behaviour change.

Years ago, I visited a large care home and caught the tail end of a training course on infectious disease control. I was there to speak with the person delivering the training, so I waited at the back. On our way to his office, the trainer and I followed a group of the trainees and watched as they returned to their ward. Only about a third of them used the antiseptic hand dispenser as they walked in the door, despite the training course they had attended a few minutes ago. I asked him how many people used to use the hand sanitiser dispensers, and he shrugged. From the trainer's point of view, he had fulfilled his obligation to train people and tick a box, but he seemed impervious to the obvious lack of behavioural change as a result of the training. This seemed to me rather bizarre.

On a more optimistic note I remember a meeting with the head of compliance of a sizeable pharmaceutical company. She was new in her post and was in the process of rethinking how they delivered on their compliance obligations. Her thinking was very different to that of the care home trainer. She came to the realisation that she might well need to run separate tracks of activity in terms of compliance training. One track would be focused on getting the various boxes ticked by delivering the type of training that conformed to the requirements of the regulatory authorities. The other track would be focused on behavioural changes so employees would be far less likely to break the regulations.

This is by no means a complete list. What are the other 'excuses' for not calling out the elephant?

Take a moment and list the barriers in your organisation to discussing and implementing effective learning transfer tools and activities. What supports those barriers and keeps them in place? How can you change the conversation? What do your colleagues say about it?

And now it's time to get tough!

How much sustainable behaviour change are you managing to achieve from the training courses you deliver? If you are like most people delivering training, the honest answer is 'not that much' or perhaps more honestly, 'I don't know'. Maybe you, as an L&D professional, can take home your salary knowing that most of the training you do is a waste of time. Maybe the people who ask for the training are happy with that low level of impact. Maybe, like some L&D people I speak with, you can bury your head in the sand or look the other way and make nonsense noises while you plug your ears with your fingers. Maybe you say some nice words about learning transfer and do a few things that might help, but really you are just doing what you have always done. Or maybe you are waking up to the reality that we should, as professionals, be doing much better than we are at producing business impact from our training courses. Given you are reading this book, I trust you are in the 'let's do better' camp and this entails providing support to the trainees to help them succeed.

There are many in L&D who would cough and splutter in indignation at the previous paragraph. How did you react? Maybe you are one of the very small minority of L&D professionals who are doing a good job of learning transfer and that paragraph genuinely does not apply to you. If so, I salute you. Or maybe you just feel very uncomfortable when someone calls out what should be obvious to all: the emperor has no clothes. In the parable of the emperor's clothes, the embarrassed ruler came to his senses and realised that he had been deceived. He had been living within an illusion where everybody was pretending something was real when even a child could see that it was not. Somehow, so many people are living within the illusion that training is working well, when even a cursory examination shows that it is in most cases not delivering on its promise.

If learning transfer is important and therefore should be done, and if it is possible to do this, and if people are avoiding it, we end up in the murky waters of responsibility and accountability. Who is responsible for making it happen, and who should be held accountable if it doesn't happen? In other words, "when and where does the buck stop?"

Stop and think for a moment about the last training course you were involved with. Who was accountable for making sure learning transfer happened? When asked that question, very few people have an answer. In other important organisational activities someone is accountable, so what's different about learning transfer?

One reason is that the activities required for successful learning transfer come from many people across different departments, and it is most unlikely that each person will do their bit and all the parts will magically coalesce into a successful programme. Somebody needs to be the conductor of the orchestra. The conductor in turn requires each member of the orchestra to play their part in the symphony. And then somebody else, perhaps whoever booked and paid for the orchestra to perform, holds the conductor accountable for the quality of the performance. So who holds the event organiser accountable? Perhaps the people who paid for tickets to attend the concert. There is inevitably a chain of accountability.

Now, think back again to the last training course you were involved with. What was, or should have been, the chain of accountability, perhaps even starting with the company shareholders or owner? Where did the chain break? If you fix that link in the chain, are there more weak links further down the chain that will then break? Take a step back and consider how accountability plays out in your organisation. Accountability is a facet of organisational culture, often driven from the top. Does the senior team take ownership? Do they accept accountability or are they full of excuses?

It is easy to say that a person should be accountable, but for delegated accountability to be effective, it must also be accepted. No-one wants to be held accountable for something that is likely to fail; that is a poisoned chalice. Alongside delegating accountability, you must also ask people if they have everything they need to be successful. If they say 'yes', then they are well on their way to accepting ownership and accountability. If they say 'no', then they will not take ownership and if/when things go wrong they will drop into spectator mode and watch as things fail. You might even get 'I told you so' comments. On the other hand, if they feel a sense of ownership because they have accepted accountability, they will step in to solve the problem when things go wrong.

Accountability is not a set-and-forget state of affairs. Each person in the accountability chain must do some 'counting'. That's the origin of the word! They should be holding regular reviews and checking the results being achieved by the person that they are holding accountable for those results. And of course, to do any of this, there must be measures in place. If you are going to hold somebody accountable for producing a specific set of results, you need to be able to measure those results to understand the level of success. In addition to defining the accountability chain, there must also be an understanding of the specifics of what each person in the chain is accountable for.

But we already
do learning transfer!

Transfer of Training – That almost magical link between classroom performance and something which is supposed to happen in the real world.

J. M. Swinney

Many L&D people I speak with say that they have taken care of the learning transfer issue and yet, when pressed, they admit that their learning transfer results are often poor and little better than just delivering the training on its own. When ask exactly what they are doing about learning transfer, here are some of the responses:

- I leave it up to the line manager
- I send them emails or text messages with facts from the training to remind them
- I give them access to a portal with lots more information
- I rely on trainees' desire to improve their performance
- I bring in coaches, either internal or external
- I set people up with support, perhaps from peers or graduates from an earlier cohort
- I run action learning sets
- I give people tasks and activities to practise and experiment
- I run a project that uses the new learning.

The most common response by far is that learning transfer is the responsibility of the line managers. This is certainly true as a statement, but learning transfer usually fails in practice unless those line managers get considerable support to operate in two different ways.

1. The line managers are responsible for the learning transfer environment that surrounds the trainee as they return to work.
2. They should also be responsible for helping the trainee implement and grow into their new skills. It is nowhere near enough for a line manager to have a few conversations after a training course.

Whatever you are doing now for learning transfer, take a good hard look and assess how successful it is. You might be doing follow-up refresher sessions, using action learning, sending out texts or emails with reminders, making more content available online, using a social media forum, or even providing coaches. Is it working? Can you prove it?

Very often these activities happen in isolation rather than being coordinated into a learning transfer workflow. What's more, the people involved are not held accountable for producing tangible and measurable results against the programme outcomes. Here is a common example: the training is nearly over and one of the traditional training rites is taking place. The trainees are being asked, in the name of learning transfer, to make a note of some actions they will take the next day, when they return to their job. You know how it goes. "Hey everybody, we're getting near to the end now, so I want you to write down a few actions you will take and some goals you aim to achieve, given all the material we have covered in the last couple of days in this workshop." And yes, I know, there are ways to make this process a bit more engaging, but something like it is happening every working day up and down the country as people start wrapping up their time in the training room. And every time it happens, whoever is paying for that training is being sold down the river.

And here's why. Whoever paid for that training had some specific business outcomes in mind, or at least hopefully they did, otherwise why were they reaching their hand into their pocket? Whether those outcomes are right or wrong, reasonable or not, they are what the paymaster is paying for. The trainee should be sent back from the course with a list of actions and goals that will deliver on the desired business outcomes being paid for. And yet, here we are, at the end of a long day in the training room, with people watching the clock and wondering when they can escape. And now they are asked to come up with their own actions and goals. I've been in that situation more than once, tired and with a head full of new and un-assimilated information, and I can't remember ever coming up with a decent goal. So, I wrote down a few things to capture some words on paper that looked as if I had thought about it. I certainly was not engaged with whatever I wrote, so it had no power beyond helping me get the day finished.

Quite apart from the lack of ability to come up with a decent goal at that point in time, there was another major problem: I never knew what the overall business outcomes of the training were, so even if I had produced a decent action or goal, one that mattered to me because of what I had experienced in the training, it probably wouldn't have been enough to fully support the business outcomes of the paymaster. If there are five key changes being sought by the organisation, it is most unlikely that each trainee will set five goals that align with those key changes, even if they care about them.

And it's not just the trainees; I doubt many of the trainers who asked me to write down goals knew those overall business outcomes either, so they couldn't guide me through the goal-setting exercise in class to get outcomes that supported the desired learning transfer. Learning transfer should be about enabling the organisational goals that the learning is designed to achieve rather than allowing brain-tired trainees to replace them or dilute them with their own personal goals, which may not have that much to do with what the organisation is looking for.

But even if you set goals that are relevant and support the true programme outcomes, how will trainees answer if you ask 'what will the consequences be if you do nothing different following the training?' If the answer is 'Nothing' or 'Nobody would notice anyway', then you have a problem. If they anticipate no consequences, good or bad, people will usually fall back into their comfort zone and do what they did before. They won't put in the time/effort/work needed to achieve their goals or implement the new learning.

And, of course, that raises the question: how much time/effort/work? Successful learning transfer flows from a philosophy of focusing on the business benefits of the learning programme rather than the learning outcomes. The entire learning programme should be treated like a business process, where the required inputs and the desired outputs from each step in the process are defined. Each process step should be designed to get those outputs, and the outputs measured where appropriate.

If you are developing a learning programme to improve, for example, report writing skills, when can you say that the programme is finished? You could argue that it is only when the report writing skills of ALL the trainees are sufficiently improved and are consistent over time that the desired business benefits have been achieved. Then you can truly say that the programme is successfully finished. This will usually be months for most learning programmes and even years for others. These timescales MUST be built into the overall learning programme design, and expectations set for all concerned.

For example, if it is decided that the training course should be a one-day workshop, how much time does the trainee need to spend, both before the workshop on getting ready and after the workshop on practising and embedding the new behaviours? Three days over six months? So, call it a four-day development programme running over six months, one day of which happens to be in the classroom. If you 'market' it as a one-day workshop, that is all the time people, both trainees and their managers, will reserve in their minds for the programme, and the lack of follow-up activity will mean it has little impact.

Over the lifecycle of a training programme, there are many people other than the trainees, their managers and the trainer who will have an interest or involvement in it – including those who will be affected by it. These are the 'stakeholders', who may be internal and/or external to the organisation. Some stakeholders may have a disproportionate influence, so it is well worth doing a stakeholder analysis to understand who are the players in the game, and their likely play. The objective of analysing stakeholders is to achieve a thorough understanding of their requirements and their interest in, and impact on, the project. The stakeholders' positions (in terms of influence and impact) may be rational and justifiable, or emotional and unfounded, but they must all be considered since, by definition, stakeholders can affect the change process and hence the programme.

Start the analysis by brainstorming a list of all the possible stakeholders. Some will fit neatly into groups, and some will not. Position them on a 2x2 matrix chart with axes 'Level of power' from low to high, and 'Level of interest' from low to high. By the way, be careful who sees this matrix as you could ruffle a few feathers if it is seen by the wrong person. The level of stakeholders' importance to the project and the potential of their impact will determine the level and type of stakeholder management activities you need to adopt. It's important to spot your influential supporters and equip them with good project information. At the very least, you will need a communications plan. This is designed to ensure that all communications address each stakeholder's particular interests, issues and needs. What you are trying to avoid are comments such as

- Why didn't you tell me...?
- Nobody told us...
- I didn't understand that...
- But we can't do that then...
- We didn't know that...

Create a communications plan specifying who needs to know what, why, when, how and how much. Make sure you are clear about who should be consulted, or at least informed before, during and after any work/stage or phase takes place.

Although, for you, the programme might be of obvious benefit and the desired results worth striving for, any change will typically generate some opposition, either active or passive, and this will take place in a political climate. It is well to heed the words of Niccolo Machiavelli from *The Prince*, "There is nothing more difficult to carry out, nor more doubtful of success, nor more dangerous to manage, than to initiate a new order of things. For the initiator has the enmity of all who would profit by the preservation of the old system, and merely lukewarm defenders in those who would gain by the new one." You need to be aware very early on of who are actively or passively against the project and find a means to neutralise them or win them over.

Successful learning transfer is as much about managing the environment and expectations surrounding a training course as it is about setting activities for people. The various stakeholders need to know what they must be prepared to contribute to the success of the programme. If they resist this commitment, the learning programme is already on shaky ground. The executive sponsor who is seeking the business benefits must step in and mandate the time commitment, for example, or the business benefits will not be realised.

Before you ever get to the point where you need to wheel out the executive sponsor to bang the drum about the programme, much needs to happen. So, let's go back to the beginning...

Where does it start?

The beginning of a book is always the hardest part for me. I'm a Chapter 3 kind of writer, which means I naturally start at Chapter 3.

Kami Garcia

Most training courses start at about Chapter 3, run for a few chapters, and then fizzle out long before the real story has ended. They are born out of discomfort or frustration with performance, so someone floats the idea that a training course is needed, and Chapter 3 is underway. Meetings are held to align the course with business needs and decide on the content that must be included. A couple of chapters later, trainees are sitting in a classroom seeing the results put together by instructional designers and subject matter experts, delivered by a skilled trainer. Reports go back to the managers interested in the story, saying the trainees rated the course highly, and the managers breathe a sigh of relief thinking the story has ended 'happily ever after'. What they haven't yet realised is that the story has not yet ended. There are many more chapters to unfold with plenty of time for the villain to interfere, and where is the hero? There's a hero? Well, there would have been one if the story had started at Chapter 1!

For your learning transfer activities to be successful, it is essential that the story of the training course, and the rationale for it, start on solid foundations. A knee-jerk training request as a response to a current or anticipated performance issue is NOT a solid foundation unless there is an effective process to verify that training is indeed a viable solution. If the training course is not seen as relevant by the participants, or the managers, it is virtually impossible to get them to put in the effort to accomplish learning transfer. Sadly, many trainees end up on training courses that have little or no perceived relationship with their real operational needs. Arguably, learning transfer starts with ensuring that the training course and the transfer of learning from it are worthwhile. This reminds me of a quote from Peter F. Drucker, "There is nothing quite so useless, as doing with great efficiency, something that should not be done at all."

Sending people on training courses that they don't need is depressingly common. It seems that L&D is often willing to ignore the need for performance diagnostics and unquestioningly accept the order for a training course. We are back to the shopkeeper mentality, and it's time greet another of the three elephants I often see in the L&D meeting room. When L&D ignores the obvious need to ascertain that a training course is required, and simply takes the order without a shred of evidence that the course will produce any business benefit, they are ignoring this elephant. I have noticed that two elephants, performance diagnostics and learning transfer, tend to travel together. In any organisation, if you find one, the other is almost sure to be lurking nearby.

The first step in addressing the performance diagnostics elephant is therefore performance consultancy. Note, this is NOT learning consultancy, which is very different. Performance consultancy starts with the premise that there is a performance gap that needs to be bridged. As we start the consultancy process, we do not assume anything about the gap or its causes, or how it could be bridged. Starting at Chapter 1 with a robust performance consultancy process protects you from delivering unsuitable training and saves considerable amounts of L&D budget. Many requests for training would never make it through the performance consultancy filter into the L&D department because the real cause of poor performance is related to the operational environment, rather than the competence of the individual performers. If someone is not performing well, there are only two things you can do to improve performance: you can either change the performer, or you can change the context within which they are performing.

The performance consultancy process applies diagnostics to the performance system to find the levers in the system that can change the output of the system. One set of levers relates to the employee: the performer. Do they have the knowledge, skills, understanding, attitude and physical attributes to do the job? In other words, are they competent? The other set of levers is to be found in the environment that surrounds that person when they are doing their job:

the context. Is the employee supplied with adequate IT, tools, management, support and so on the do their job? In other words, is the work environment 'competent'? I find it extraordinary that we go to sometimes inordinate lengths to build competency frameworks for people, yet we don't do this for the environment within which they are working. For a full performance consultancy process, see *Capability at Work: How to Solve the Performance Puzzle* by Paul Matthews (2014).

David McClelland's team at Harvard summarised the requirements for any significant change to be lasting and effective as follows: people must
- be willing to change (if they're not, it's a motivation issue)
- be able to change (if they're not, it's a training/competency issue)
- not be prevented from changing (if they are, it's a 'systemic' issue).

When you have found the levers within the performance system, you need to consider which ones to pull, and in which order. Consider the costs of pulling each one, how quickly you can pull that lever to find out how it affects the system in practice, how the effects of pulling different levers are interdependent, and so on. Often, the first step will be some tests to find out the sensitivity of the performance system to specific levers.

Of the dozens of possible levers, it is highly unlikely that the only levers you will find are a lack of knowledge and/or skills, which means that your programme to improve knowledge and skills needs to work in tandem with other projects involving other levers. It is also often the case that you will find these knowledge and skills levers need no improvement at all, which means that you do NOT need a training programme to improve them, no matter how much noise your operational managers might be making as they request training programmes for their poorly performing team. In my experience, and that of others I speak with, around 80% of performance problems are caused by organisational and environmental barriers – in other words, environmental incompetence, rather than worker incompetence.

Think back to your own experience over the last month. Which tasks on your to-do list did you fail to do adequately? In other words, when did you underperform? Of those times, how many were because of your lack of knowledge or skill? How many were the result of outside influence? Was your underperformance correctable by further training? Even if the answer to that is yes, would training be a reasonable way to correct that?

Another test I have heard mentioned, though I wouldn't try this for real, is to imagine one of the underperformers. If you threatened them by pointing a gun at their head, could they do the job? If they could, it means they know how to do it and can do it, so it's not a training issue.

If, and only if, the diagnostics show that one of the levers you can pull is to improve knowledge and skills (and perhaps after you have tried pulling a few lower-cost levers just in case that will be sufficient to get the change you want), can you then move to the next stage of setting up a learning intervention. You MUST be absolutely certain that the knowledge/skills lever is worth spending money on. What's your proof that it is? Why that lever? If you don't have proof, return to your performance diagnostics process and go through it again. Management should not allow programmes to proceed unless the benefit to the business can be clearly articulated. Likewise, L&D professionals should not accept the responsibility for conducting a programme unless the business benefits are clear to both line and learning managers.

Please go back and read that last paragraph again. It will save you a LOT of money.

OK, now we can move on. The next step is learning consultancy. This starts with the premise, proven by the performance consultancy diagnostics, that there is a knowledge/skills gap we need to bridge, and that a learning intervention, probably alongside other changes, is needed to solve the presenting performance issue. The learning experts should now be looking at the whole picture to design a learning programme that

- fulfils the learning needs identified in the performance consultancy process
- aligns with both the strategic and tactical needs of the business
- fits within the budget
- includes learning transfer activities
- includes enough measurement to check that it's working as designed.

The instructional designers can now get to work with their well-established models, such as ADDIE, to design suitable learning interventions. It is worth remembering at this stage to differentiate between information that trainees must 'know' and information they can 'find'. With so much information readily available online, there is little point in attempting to get people to remember what they can look up easily. Regardless of whether they need to 'know it' or 'find it', the desire to drive learning transfer should permeate all design decisions for every element of the programme. After all, without learning transfer, most formal learning efforts are wasted.

A word of caution: it is very important that you do not get performance consultancy mixed up with learning consultancy. They are two different things and spring from two different assumptions. Performance consultancy starts from the assumption that there is a performance gap, and the diagnostics process is to identify the causes of that gap. Learning consultancy starts from the assumption that there is a knowledge/skills gap and seeks to design effective ways to bridge that gap.

I have spoken with many L&D professionals who claim to do performance consultancy based on the fact that they 'align' their learning solutions with the needs of the business. They are wrong. They are looking at a performance problem with the assumption that there will be a learning solution. From this basic assumption, they cannot do performance consultancy, they can only do learning consultancy.

In a sense, this is malpractice in the same way that you would accuse a doctor of malpractice if they assume that prescribing antibiotics is the solution for any health issue that their patients present. The performance consultant, like the doctor, must start with an open mind.

Informal learning

*I don't divide the world into the weak and the strong, or the successes
and the failures... I divide the world into the learners and non-learners.*

Benjamin Barber

Informal learning has a major role in learning transfer, yet this role is mostly ignored. It is vastly more important than you'd ever think given the way we usually carry out learning, training and other staff development. In most organisations, informal learning is the third elephant in the room because, despite the popularity of the 70:20:10 model, people still do very little to utilise the huge proportion of learning that is informal. They may at least talk about 70:20:10, but then often carry on delivering L&D services in much the same way as they always did, perhaps with some extra blended approaches. If you look at what they are actually doing, you wouldn't recognise much that will effectively make use of the enormous power of the informal learning elephant.

There are many models and theories of learning that try to explain the incredibly complex process of learning. Learning is a process that has evolved within us as we, in turn, evolved to become homo sapiens. It is such an integral part of who we are and what we do that we are to a large extent not even aware that we are learning unless we look back on situations in hindsight.

If you ask the scientists and academics involved with learning research, they will give you models and theories, although none of these seem to be the one model that rules them all. If you are interested in the various models, visit the website www.learning-theories.com for a list of the learning theories, with simple and easy-to-read summaries. But if you ask most people how they learn something, they will say they learn by doing it, and by practising it. Even if they know the theory, it remains abstract until they put it into practice and discover how it works for them in their world, in their context. Proficiency and performance grow out of practice and experience. Ask yourself and think of your own experience. How did you come to learn what you know in order to do your current job? A lot of extra understanding is available when information is applied in a real-life situation, and that understanding evolves as the situation provides feedback over multiple iterations.

In fact, think of everything you have ever learned. You learned most of it through life, through living. You could almost say that learning is an unavoidable, and thankfully desirable, side effect of life. Without our ability to learn as we live, we would have been consigned to the evolutionary dustbin a long time ago. How did you learn to run a household? I'll bet you didn't go to formal classes on it, and yet here you are running a household with at least some level of proficiency. It is virtually impossible for us to imagine a world without informal learning. Learning for us is such a fundamental part of our existence that we usually don't even notice it, any more than we notice the air we breathe. People are learning all the time; without that learning, organisations would be dead in the water within months, and probably even just weeks.

Learners, especially adult learners, develop their behaviour according to their experiences, not teaching. This was first highlighted by John Dewey as far back as 1938, along with his contemporaries Kurt Lewin and Jean Piaget. His ideas were built upon by others, including David Kolb. Adults do not learn in the same ways as children do, therefore applying the learning theories of pedagogy to adults is a mistake. Adults already have a great deal of prior experience which they build on, and usually they wish to learn because of a pressing need. In other words, they respond to pressures in their professional lives and seek to find rapid and practical solutions. This means they won't always look for a teacher, or a course, and this results in informal learning.

Informal learning is not some new-fangled thing, but we are still not really leveraging what it can do for us in an organisational context. Generally, informal learning is not directed by anybody. It is a natural response to observing others, having conversations, trying things out and reflecting on experiences. It is triggered as a result of what's going on, or it might be triggered by ad hoc researching of relevant blogs, videos, articles and so on as people seek to understand what is going on or find out what they need to know to accomplish something. For more information on informal learning, including case studies, see *Informal Learning at Work: How to Boost Performance in Tough Times* by Paul Matthews (2013).

In terms of learning transfer, a significant amount of informal learning MUST take place after a training course, if the training course is to have any impact on performance and business results. To get the benefits, we must realise that classroom learning is only a small part of the total learning workflow that is required if the organisation is to benefit from the new knowledge and skills introduced by the training programme. The learning workflow must continue well beyond the learning event that occurred in the classroom and include structured application, experimentation and practice. How are people ever going to get good at something if they don't practise?

Think of learning transfer as a process that moves systematically from classroom instruction to closely-supervised application in practice assignments and then to increasingly independent application in real work settings, but with some degree of ongoing support. That is, transfer of learning is facilitated by a process of systematically decreasing support and increasing the real-world nature of the application contexts. Transfer should never be assumed, but rather planned for within a learning workflow designed to embed new skills and behaviours.

Informal learning as a component of learning transfer is a special case, or if you like subset, of informal learning, because it needs to be focused on some specific outcomes rather than the way most informal learning happens, which is coincidental. When it comes to learning transfer, the required informal learning often doesn't happen, because it is not triggered anywhere near frequently enough, or in the right way. If we want to generate informal learning that is focused on the training course material, we must find some way of triggering it, and directing it. Our goal is to reduce the time to proficiency and therefore we need to accelerate and intensify the informal learning inherent in experience, rather than wait for the universe to haphazardly provide the necessary experience. Therein lies part of the problem.

Informal learning is very powerful, but its power comes largely from its informality and from its place within the flow of our lives. When we seek to direct it, we can kill its power by killing its informality, separating it from the natural flow of our lives. So then we need to ask how we can direct informal learning without rendering it powerless. How can we tap into its power for specific learning outcomes to support and extend our formal learning event, rather than the happenstance outcomes that usually result from its informality? It seems to me that we need a halfway house where we can 'manage' informal learning, but with a light touch that does not destroy it. It is like 'managing' a butterfly you hold in your cupped hands. Too tight, and you kill the butterfly. Too loose, and the butterfly escapes, and you have no influence over it at all.

By and large, informal learning happens through activities, through people doing things or observing things, and then reflecting on those things. That reflection is magnified if they discuss those things with somebody else. Therefore, create a process to delegate activities that have been carefully designed to trigger the desired reflection and learning, and then debrief those activities to get the magnification effect.

The Learning Stack

By three methods we may learn wisdom: first, by reflection, which is noblest; second, by imitation, which is easiest; and third by experience, which is the bitterest.

Confucius

One of the critical success factors for learning is reflection. According to the constructivist model of learning, people play an active role in constructing their understanding and knowledge of the world through reflection. They use reflection to embed their new information within their existing concepts and experiences. Indeed, most people would agree that learning cannot take place without some level of reflection. Lev Vygotsky, the pioneer of social constructivism in learning, talked about "consciousness being formed by communication". In other words, reflecting on and then explaining what you have done, are doing and intend to do next becomes a significant learning activity in its own right.

This has significant consequences for understanding and creating the conditions under which people learn most effectively. It's not enough to tell people about a concept, skill or behaviour, they also need opportunities to experience these, and then reflect on their experience to incorporate them into their model of the world. For example, I might intellectually understand the steps in a negotiation model, but until I sit across the table from someone and use that model in the real world, I don't really 'know' it. And until I practise that model many times in many different situations, I won't be able to use it as fluently as an expert. Experts learn their expertise through experience, reflection and deliberate practice.

Let's look at how we can use this to underpin the thinking for a learning intervention and the subsequent learning transfer. I have developed a very simple model with five levels of reflection that I call the 'Learning Stack'. The higher up the levels you can push the learner in terms of the quality and quantity of the reflection, the more likely it is the learning will stick, and be transferred into behavioural change.

1. Unconscious reflection

   I know 'unconscious reflection' sounds like an oxymoron, but it occurs when we practise something and improve our performance without consciously reflecting on what we need to do to improve. We have an unconscious targeting mechanism that guides us towards improvement. This 'practice makes perfect' process is very evident when we practise physical skills, such as driving or typing or sports skills.

2. Conscious reflection

   This is what we normally regard as reflection – where we consider what happened. Note that for this type of reflection to be useful from a learning perspective, it needs to be questions-based. We need to be asking ourselves how things could be different, who can do it better, how do they do it and so on. Simply reflecting on how well, or how badly, you did something has little effect without a questioning overlay.

3. External reflection

   If we take our thoughts and externalise them to a journal, a colleague, or even the dog, we need to re-formulate the disorganised content of our internal processing into a sequence of ideas and language that the outside world can understand. This 'translation' for external consumption adds another level to our thinking and engages larger areas of our neural network.

4. External reflection with consequences

   When we think there may be consequences to us of externalising our reflection, or if we think someone will judge us based on what we put out there, we will think twice. It adds another layer of reflection when we try to imagine what someone else will think about us if we share our reflection with a coach or a boss, or in a blog or an email.

5. Teaching someone else

   I am sure you have heard the aphorism that the best way to learn something is to teach it. I believe it is more accurate to say that the best way to learn something is to prepare the lesson plan with which to teach it. It is the reflection on how to prepare and present the material to novices that deepens understanding, rather than the presentation itself.

Level four is a result of what social scientists term the 'audience effect'. There have been some fascinating experiments on this effect in which students were asked to put their English homework on a blog rather than just hand it in to their teacher. The extra level of exposure their homework received caused them to improve their standards considerably. This is well explained in *Smarter Than You Think* by Clive Thompson, where he cites a range of experiments and research. He sums it up on page 55: "The effort of communicating to someone else forces you to think more precisely, make deeper connections, and learn more." This clarity through expression is one of the reasons communities of practice are successful and valued by experts. A community of practice provides a context in which people reflect, reinforce and extend their knowledge by discussing it with each other.

Although this 'Learning Stack' is a very simplistic view of a complex process, it is useful. For any learning intervention, consider how far up this learning stack you are pushing the learners. For example, if you give them something to read you are pushing them to level 2. In the classroom, when you generate discussion between the trainees, you are pushing them to level 3. When they are debriefed on an activity by their manager or a coach, you are pushing them to level 4 and so on. The level of reflection correlates with understanding and recall. This has implications in terms of the amount of time it takes for someone to reach proficiency, not just in relation to how far up the learning stack they have been pushed, but also how frequently they are on the learning stack in relation to a specific set of skills. By exposing learners to a systematically organised set of situations in a compressed timeframe, they experience what might otherwise take years to accumulate.

It is also worth considering this alongside the way that memory works. When we consider learning in its most abstract form, we can think of it as occurring in three related phrases. The first is encoding, the second is consolidation, and the third is retrieval. Encoding refers to how marks on a page or sounds in the air can be translated into something that can be stored in the brain. Consolidation is the actual storage process, which is the modification, over the short or long term, of neural activity within the brain to support memory. Finally, retrieval is the pulling out or accessing of previously-learned information. What is interesting here is that our traditional learning efforts tend to be focused on encoding and consolidation, when our end goal is retrieval. Sure, we must get the information input and memorise it in the first place, but if we cannot retrieve it reliably, it is useless to us.

Our ability to retrieve information is affected by how often we retrieve it, so a good learning strategy is retrieval practice. Each act of retrieval or recall causes further elaboration of that information and generates stronger consolidation, which in turn makes it easier to recall it again later. The frequency of retrieval seems to signal to the mind the relative importance of the information and thus how readily it will need to be retrieved again in the future. Retrieval practice is probably the most effective way of learning, so any activities following a training course that require recall will help cement the learning in place. There is one caveat here though: what we retrieve is not identical to what we originally encoded and stored. It is a compilation that is created on the fly during retrieval from the current context and the available retrieval cues. What we encode and store is not a verbatim like-for-like representation of what we experienced. It may feel like this to us, but our brain is fooling us. I am sure you have heard about cases where several eye witnesses described the getaway car differently. If we encourage retrieval, but don't correct a retrieved compiled memory that is false, we will embed that false 'memory' more strongly than the original input. Retrieval appears to modify the memory in anticipation of how we might need it in the future. This is one of the problems with exams. In a high-pressure exam, with stress neurochemicals on the march, what is retrieved is remembered, and yet in a typical exam it is not corrected if it is wrong. Unless the student is answering questions 100% correctly, they are actually 'learning/embedding' incorrect information that is likely to outlast and 'trump' the correct information the next time that subject is recalled.

Here are some strategies that you can use to facilitate retrieval-based learning.
- Enhance metacognition. Many people predict that if they simply re-study material, it will increase retention. But this is not the most effective approach. Help learners to see that a more effective strategy for enhancing learning and long-term retention is to repeatedly practise recalling the information one has studied.
- Practise with a range real-world scenarios. Studies show the importance of context in retrieval: when participants repeatedly retrieve knowledge in a testing environment, they perform better on the test. Information can, however, become 'context-bound'

when taught with limited context-specific examples. It makes sense, then, to ensure a wide range of simulations or real-world scenarios in practice.

- Provide multiple self-checks and exercises. Since repeated recall has been shown to increase long-term retention, provide multiple opportunities for learners to test themselves for critical information, even when they have proven they know the material. (Of course, most learners would not bother with a second self-check activity unless they were informed about the effectiveness of retrieval-based learning.)
- Provide opportunities for group discussions. After a learning event, take advantage of discussions with colleagues, fellow trainees or a coach/manager that facilitate the recall of critical knowledge. Set the discussions up to include focused questioning.

Reflection on and recall of a memory modifies it in terms of how it is stored for future retrieval. Memories are not like documents we keep in computers or file boxes. We don't simply make them once and store them. Instead, we grow our memories as we develop them into sets of complex neural connections. This takes time. Once some neural changes have occurred, we can go back and embed the learning by practising the use of our new neural connections. This strengthens their interconnectivity and the way they are organised. Experts tend to organise their stored knowledge based on the categories of problems for which that knowledge can be used, whereas a recent graduate has their knowledge organised and encoded in a way that is similar to a textbook. As graduates gain experience and recall the knowledge for use, it reorganises, or perhaps it might be better to say, it gets re-indexed for easier future retrieval, based on how it is more likely to be used in the future. This, in turn, improves the way they interpret information from their environment, particularly in spotting patterns that a novice would not notice, and improves their ability to remember, reason, and solve problems. This suggests that the way you organise the delivery of content within the training room will have an impact on how useful it will be later in the workplace, and how easy it will be to transfer.

In the *NeuroLeadership Journal* (2014)[8], Josh Davis and colleagues published an update to their AGES model, 'The Science of Making Learning Stick'.

---

[8] Davis, Balda, Rock, McGinniss and Davachi, *NeuroLeadership Journal* (Vol 5, August 2014), 'The Science of Making Learning Stick: An Update to the AGES Model'

Their neuroscience-based AGES model was developed originally in 2010 and suggests four principles that embed new learning so that it sticks. The four principles summarize the big drivers of memory systems in the brain during encoding: there must be sufficient attention (A) on the new material; learners must generate (G) their own connections to knowledge that they already have; moderate levels of emotion (E) are necessary, and coming back to the information regularly – spacing (S) – works wonders. According to Davis et al., the essential ingredients of learning are those factors that create optimal conditions for one brain region, called the hippocampus, to do its job. It registers those experiences that are to be remembered when they occur, and then later re-activates the relevant brain regions in appropriate synchrony across the whole cortex, facilitating recall of those memories. There are ways to leverage Attention, Generation, Emotion and Spacing to help the hippocampus perform optimally.

(A) There are three things about the relationship between attention and learning that are central to optimizing learning.
1. Attention has limits of only about 20 minutes before needing a refresher.
2. Multitasking is the enemy of learning because the brain uses rapid task switching rather than genuine multitasking. Ironically, people who self-report that they are good at multitasking are usually worse performers of it than people who don't. Trying to practise it to get good at it only makes it worse because it speeds up the task switching and makes each mini-period of focus shallower.
3. Attention is especially susceptible to interference with materials of the same modality (such as reading language and hearing language). In other words, don't speak until the trainees have read your slide, or just use a relevant picture on the slide and then you can speak over it.

(G) Generation is the act of creating internal connections to new or presented ideas. Importantly, it is the act of generation that matters and not whether the connections that are made are brilliant. Think of it as welcoming the new idea into your mind and introducing it to its new neighbours. Insight, that eureka moment when the unconscious mind solves a problem, is perhaps the most valuable form of generation. Insights are the result of wide-scale reorganisation of the elements of a problem into a new and previously non-obvious solution. Insight is directly related to generation by connecting ideas in a way they have not been previously connected. Generation is the underpinning for the success of level 5 reflection in the learning stack. Teaching, or even mentally preparing to teach an idea, is such a sure-fire way to generate new connections and thus deep learning that we would be remiss not to take advantage of it whenever we can.

(E) It turns out that levels of emotional arousal matter for making learning last, although too much can be distracting and therefore counterproductive. Think back to experiences you remember well. There was probably a significant emotional component at the time, but 'flat' experiences don't last so long in our memory. With emotional arousal, the hippocampus gets additional signals from brain regions that respond to arousing stimuli, and this helps to activate the hippocampus to the point where it can do its job more effectively. Both positive and negative emotions have an impact on memory retention, but positive is preferable because it is harder to over-arouse a positive emotion. Positive emotions can facilitate other factors helpful for learning, such as insight and social collaboration.

(S) Spacing: having some space (usually a day or more) between learning and review sessions is the most counterintuitive and yet perhaps most important of the four learning principles. People think that cramming the learning into a marathon session works. However, one study found that 90% of participants had better longer-term memory performance after spacing. Despite this result, 72% of the participants reported that cramming was more effective than spacing. Perhaps the myth about cramming comes from our experiences of successfully cramming the night before a test in which short-term memory was rewarded, while longer-term retention was mostly irrelevant. Within a study session, a spacing of a few minutes with a distracting filler task is useful, and for longer spacing, a period that involves sleep is ideal. Sleeping provides optimal conditions for processes that integrate newly-encoded memories into long-term storage. Sleep not only helps the brain to strengthen memories, but also to actively forget irrelevant information, thus optimizing memory for what is relevant.

Think about the learning stack and the way memory works in terms of learning transfer. Learners need to do new things after training and reflect on their experiences. They also need to get plenty of practice recalling information within an environment that offers correction when they make mistakes while practising using the information. So, how do we get them doing new things related to what they have learnt? Sometimes, and I mean only sometimes, they will do new things simply because they now know how to do them, they think it's a good idea to do them after being on the training course, and their environment does not stifle their desire to do the new thing or stop them doing it. It is far more likely, however, that whatever you want them to do differently after the training course will require the learner practising, experimenting, and going through a reflective process to try and use their newfound classroom-generated knowledge and embed it into their own work context. This will not happen spontaneously. They will need prompts to trigger the behaviours of doing the practice and experimentation, and then reflecting on it.

Triggers that work

Knowing is not enough; we must apply. Willing is not enough; we must do.

Johann Wolfgang von Goethe

BJ Fogg is a behavioural psychologist, author, and founder and director of the Stanford Behaviour Design Lab. He has developed the concept of 'Behaviour Design', which comprises a set of models for understanding how human behaviour works, as well as a set of methods to help influence it.

According to Fogg, three specific elements must converge at the same moment for a specific behaviour to occur. Given that learning transfer is only successful when the learner starts behaving in the desired new ways, Fogg's work is critical to understanding how to generate these new behaviours. The Fogg Behavioural Model states that B=MAP. That is, a specific behaviour will occur if at the same moment there are sufficient motivation, sufficient ability and a sufficient prompt. If the behaviour does not occur, at least one of these three elements is missing.

The prompt is, in effect, a call to action to do a specific behaviour. The prompt must be 'loud' enough for the target person to perceive it and be consciously aware of it. Once aware of a prompt, the target immediately, and largely unconsciously, assesses their ability to carry out the requested behaviour: how difficult would this be, how long will it take, who can help me, and so on. They base this on their perception of the difficulty of the requested behaviour, and their ability, as they see it, to achieve that behaviour. They balance this against their motivation to respond to the call to action. If, in that moment, their motivation is high enough for them to attempt the behaviour, given their assessment of its difficulty, they will make a start. The prompt will succeed, and the behaviour will occur. If their motivation is not high enough, then the prompt will fail.

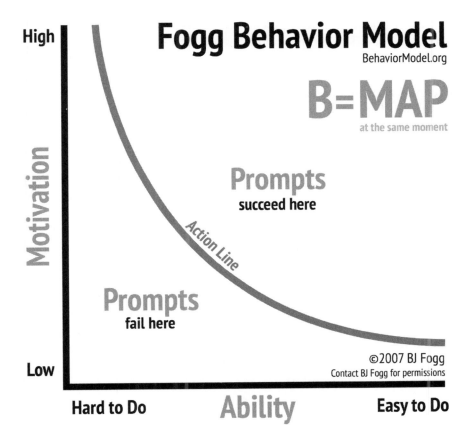

Notice that the bottom axis of the graph is all about perception rather than reality. It is the person presented with a prompt who decides whether the requested behaviour is hard or easy, regardless of what someone else might think. This is why the same prompt will work for one person and not necessarily for another.

Deployment of learning after a training course requires the trainees to do something that is different from what they were doing before the training course. That is, a new behaviour is required, and this means it needs to be triggered. The triggering prompt could be very explicit and direct, such as an email request to do a task or practise a skill. It could also be implicit and indirect, such as the expectation that, if a set of circumstances arises, the trainee should use something they have learned in a training course. And anything in between.

If the trigger is direct, then we have control over the form and timing of the prompt. We can design the prompt carefully to make sure that it is seen or heard. Email? Text? An item on a checklist? How? We can also design the prompt to include information that could increase the motivation of the target person by making sure they have a big enough 'Why should I do this?' The timing of the prompt is also important. Can we set the prompt to occur for a certain task when the trainee is more likely to be in a sufficient state of motivation for the task? There is likely to be a 'honeymoon' period after a training course, when the memory of the ideas and excitement about the possibilities are still fresh in the trainee's mind. How long this honeymoon period will last is typically dependent on the attitude and support they get from their manager and peers when they are back at their desk. Also consider the time of the day and the day of the week they will receive the prompt. When are the trainees most likely to be able to accept and respond to a prompt positively?

However, if the prompt is implicit in a set of circumstances, we must ensure that those circumstances will be recognised by the trainee within their own context and they will be easily able to spot that scenario as it unfolds. If the scenario is not always obvious, an alternative is to set up prompts for the behaviour of testing for the scenario until that becomes habitual. Look at the prompts you are relying on. Where are they on the continuum from implicit to explicit? How can you improve each prompt?

In addition to prompt design, we can also design the requested behaviour or task so that it appears small and easy to do. All other things being equal, the smaller the task appears, the more likely it is that the prompt will succeed. This suggests that many small tasks are more likely to succeed than a few big ones, even if the cumulative effect is the same.

On his website www.foggmethod.com, Fogg outlines his three steps for changing behaviour:
1. Get specific
2. Make it easy
3. Trigger the behaviour

Within each of these steps he includes ideas and tools to accomplish the steps, which are not as simplistic as they might seem at first glance. He also offers the following as some common approaches to behaviour change that don't work well (and I confess I have used some of these in the past):

1. Present information and hope it leads to attitude change and then behaviour change
2. Give people a big goal and then focus on increasing motivation or sustaining willpower
3. Move people through psychological stages until they are ready to change
4. Assume all behaviours are the result of choices
5. Make persuasion techniques, such as scarcity or reciprocity, the starting point for your solution.

I would recommend that you watch Fogg's TEDx talk on YouTube *Forget big change, start with a tiny habit* (Dec, 2012) and visit his sites http://behaviormodel.org and www.bjfogg.com for more detailed information on how to work with the three elements, MAP, to ensure a behaviour occurs.

Another model that comes into play here is the Comfort, Stretch, Panic model. It is often attributed to Karl Rohnke, but is probably founded on the Yerkes-Dodson law, which dictates that performance increases with physiological or mental arousal, but only up to a point. When levels of arousal become too high, performance decreases. The Comfort, Stretch, Panic model is often represented as three concentric circles with the inner circle being the comfort zone, the middle circle being the stretch zone, and the outer circle being the panic zone.

If you are asked to do an activity, which zone does it fall into? And how do you react to tasks in the different zones? Do you gravitate towards comfortable tasks because, well, they are comfortable? Do you gravitate towards stretch tasks because you are more likely to find excitement and learning there? How do you cope if you find you have to do a task that for you is in the panic zone?

It's also worth considering how these zones grow and shrink over time as we gain experience and our perception of our skills changes. If we spend almost all our time in the comfort zone, it is likely the zone will shrink as we become less confident in tackling anything that is in any way new or different. If we spend time in the stretch zone where we find novelty, exploration and adventure, it will probably expand the boundaries of both the comfort zone and the stretch zone. It is not really a comfortable place, but it is stimulating as we challenge ourselves to perform better and do more. If we spend too much time in the panic zone, we may get burned to the point that we retreat to the comfort zone to lick our wounds.

The idea of introducing learning tasks in the stretch zone, and thereby introducing some level of anxiety, is different to other learning theories, which posit that a fully supportive and non-anxious environment is more conducive to learning. Our reaction to these zones is idiosyncratic. Do we tend to yearn for adventure and learning, or do we prefer to stick to what we know so that we don't fail?

In part, this is based on our reaction to what we think might change, and how that change will affect us. Anxiety, after all, is the fear we have when we imagine a future event not turning out as well as we hope, causing us to lose something we value. Think of a change you were afraid of, or just worried about. Was it really the change that was generating the fear? Or was it your thinking about the possible losses you might suffer because of the change?

Notice that the fear is due to anticipating loss. Fear is about imagining a future event turning out badly so that, as a result, we suffer loss. So that begs the question, why would we imagine something in the future going wrong? The answer seems to be related to the locus of control. If we feel that we are fully in control of the situation, and the change, then we can 'make' it go well, and avoid any loss. We have no fear when we believe that we are fully in control. As the locus of control moves outside us, or outside people we trust, then we fear in proportion to the probability and magnitude of the potential loss. And of course, everyone is different in terms of how much they react to the potential for loss. Some are more laid back by nature, and some are more anxious.

Dr Robert Maurer in his book *One Small Step Can Change your Life: The Kaizen Way* (May 2014) posits that the human brain co-operates with low-key change. Maurer maintains that for most people, change is frightening and therefore the key to change is to take small steps in a non-threatening way or environment so that fear is circumnavigated. The fear itself is generated by the amygdala, which creates a chemical storm that shuts down the cortex of the brain, together with rational and creative thinking and anything else that could interfere with the physical ability to run or fight. The problem is, rational and creative thinking are just what you need to do the new and different tasks involved with change. With small goals, we are in control; the fear is bypassed; the amygdala sleeps, and change is possible.

One of the things that moves the locus of control outside us, waking up the amygdala, is if we are uncertain about our ability to cope with the change. Do we have the knowledge and skills to handle the change and stay 'in control'? If not, can we get the right kind of support on demand to enable us to cope with the change? If we don't have the abilities needed to manage/control the change, can we learn them fast enough?

Our perception of our abilities, which includes whether we believe we are capable of improving those abilities when needed, has a massive effect on how we cope with the idea of change, of doing something new, and the fear of possible loss. Our mindset matters when we are presented with a call to perform a new behaviour or are confronted with a goal that pushes us into our stretch zone or beyond.

Mindset

*One can choose to go back toward safety or forward toward growth.
Growth must be chosen again and again; fear must be overcome again
and again.*

Abraham Maslow

Carol S. Dweck is a professor of psychology at Stanford University in the USA. She has been researching the field of achievement and success for decades, and has created a new psychology of success, based on mindset.

Dweck's book *Mindset – The New Psychology of Success: Changing the Way You Think to Fulfil Your Potential* (2006) is, in my opinion, a must-read for anybody in learning or education. The first three chapters give you a good grounding of her model without the jargon so often found in academic writing. The following chapters are rich with stories on how her mindset model plays out in the arenas of sport, education, work, and relationships. It explains the significant role mindset played in the collapse of Enron under Jeffrey Skilling and the success of General Electric under Jack Welch. For a shortcut to understand Dweck's approach, watch the TEDx video on YouTube by Eduardo Briceno, *The Power of belief -- mindset and success* (Nov, 2012).

In the introduction, Dweck describes her book thus: "In this book, you'll learn how a simple belief about yourself – a belief we discovered in our research – guides a large part of your life. In fact, it permeates *every* part of your life. Much of what you think of as your personality actually grows out of this 'mindset'. Much of what may be preventing you from fulfilling your potential grows out of it." I think the book does even more than she claims it does – especially for those of us in L&D who can use her model as a lens to look at both learning in general and learning transfer in particular.

As I was working on this section of the book, quite by chance I watched a short video on the BBC website about the first woman to become a minibus driver in Cairo. She began driving to make a living after her husband died. She told the interviewer (while driving, of course), "I wanted a way to support myself, and to be able to raise my children. I decided on driving. Driving is a good job, and I love it." She had never driven a minibus before this. "I told them I would learn. Nothing is too hard to do." What an amazing attitude towards learning, and what a shame not all of us have it. In Dweck's model, this is termed a 'growth mindset', one that takes the view that your capacities, your abilities, your talents are malleable and that they can be improved through directed, focused and attentive practice. By contrast, at the other end of the continuum, a 'fixed mindset' suggests that your talents, your abilities and your capacities are fixed. In other words, they are immutable and do not change as a result of practice.

Those of us with a fixed mindset tend to work on the basis that we were dealt a hand of cards by the universe when we were born in terms of our ability and talents. We get to play those cards as best we can, and if we were lucky, we got some good cards. We see our abilities and talents as relatively fixed, and although we believe we can learn things, we 'know' that there are limits to how good we could ever become. Have you ever heard someone say, 'I'm rubbish at singing! Even if you gave me lessons, I could never be a singer. It's just not in me.' Those of us with a growth mindset, in contrast, tend to work on the basis that we can get better at anything, and we can improve our ability and talents if we choose to do so. It just takes some effort.

As you read about those two mindsets, how did you react? Did one leave you a bit puzzled, as though it didn't make sense? Did the other seem such an obvious statement that you are wondering why I am even writing about it? People with each mindset find it virtually impossible to understand the world view of the opposite mindset.

Those with a fixed mindset will be automatically seeking to avoid failure, or more specifically, being seen to fail. For someone with a fixed mindset, failure is like a permanent condition. It is like a tattoo on their forehead that says 'FAILURE'. A fixed mindset person regards failure as a measure of the boundaries of their abilities. Failure tells them they have overextended beyond their ability, and since their mindset suggests that ability is fixed, they can never succeed beyond those boundaries. Fixed mindset people seek to stay within their perception of their ability boundaries, so they can avoid failure and maintain a sense of being smart and skilled. They would prefer not to try, rather than try and fail. They therefore deliberately underestimate their abilities to ensure they stay within their comfort zone, where they know they can succeed. They want certainty of success before proceeding. A corollary to this is that they have a small stretch zone. If you push them slightly outside their comfort zone, to the point where failure becomes a possibility, the potential for 'loss' pushes them rapidly onwards into their panic zone.

On the other hand, those with a growth mindset will usually relish a new challenge if it is in an area where they wish to improve. They don't mind failure because they see it as the gateway to improvement and a springboard for growth. For them, failure is a temporary condition, a puzzle to be solved, and nothing to be ashamed of. Failure to them just means they need to practice more and put in more effort so they can improve and ultimately succeed in doing what needs to be done. Short-term failure is acceptable, and even desirable as a learning experience; long-term failure isn't really considered because they know that with some more work they will reach success.

Note that people can have different mindsets towards different aspects of their lives; for example, they may have a fixed mindset concerning their ability to sing, but a growth mindset concerning their ability to do maths. Despite this, according to Dweck, most of us tend to be evenly split as either one or the other across most contexts in our lives, though there is a group of about 20% of us who are a mix of the two. The consequences of living with either of these mindsets are profound. Out of these two mindsets springs a great deal of our behaviour, our relationship with success and failure in both professional and personal contexts, and ultimately our capacity for happiness. I find it interesting that people tend to think that they have more of a growth mindset than they display in their actual thinking and behaviour. As an example, I have heard people talk about their growth mindset, yet they become defensive when receiving feedback, or they feel threatened or intimidated by others' success. It is easier to say that we believe in the ability to learn and grow than it is to consistently display the thinking and behaviour that truly reflect that belief.

I suggest you read Dweck's book for the bigger picture: whether it is nature or nurture and how to change your own mindset. In this book, let's focus on how the two mindsets play out within the context of learning transfer. We have already established that implementing new learning in the workflow, and thereby accomplishing learning transfer, will require people to start behaving differently. These new behaviours need to be prompted by a call to action, and it is the reaction to that prompt in terms of an assessment of personal ability and current motivation that will govern whether the behaviour will happen or not. The key word here is 'personal', because each person will be assessing both their motivation and their ability through the lens of their own mindset.

Trainees with a fixed mindset, and therefore a strong performance orientation, seek to achieve better scores. They are anxious about their ability to achieve better scores and therefore avoid engagement in situations in which they may fail. They want to be perceived as capable and thus may learn less during training. In contrast, trainees with a strong learning orientation seek to acquire new skills and master any novel situation. Individuals with a learning mindset exert more effort in learning, engage in more adaptive and flexible thinking strategies, stay on task after receiving feedback, and demonstrate stronger learning outcomes.

There is also some evidence that an individual's mindset determines the way they will respond to different types of training. Those with a stronger learning mindset may demonstrate poorer performance during training, as they are more prone to take risks and learn from their mistakes. However, they outperform others on retention and transfer tasks because they learn trained principles at a deeper level. In addition, trainees with a stronger learning/growth mindset tend to learn best from training that allows them more control over the way they explore and organise training material. For instance, they respond positively to difficult goals and opportunities to self-regulate during training. By contrast, trainees with a fixed mindset may respond negatively to these same training features. Such individuals seem to learn best in a highly-structured environment, in which they complete successively more difficult tasks.

Clearly, when trying something new, those with a fixed mindset require a lot more support, along with reassurance that not getting things quite right when they are practising is okay and to be expected. You can even suggest that you are bringing out a nascent skill as opposed to asking them to learn something totally new, which would scare them. Those with a growth mindset, on the other hand, may need some careful managing if the consequences of failure while they are practising are significant to the business, as they may have a cavalier attitude towards risk. How people interpret challenges, setbacks and criticism is their choice. They can interpret them with a fixed mindset as signs that their inherent talents or abilities are lacking, or they can interpret them with a growth mindset as signs that they need to ramp up their strategies and effort, stretch themselves, and expand their abilities.

Dweck did some fascinating experiments on the way that linguistic queues within feedback given by teachers to students affected the way the students behaved following the feedback. A paper published in 2007 by Dweck, Blackwell and colleagues described an experiment in which teachers praised a particular trait with a comment such as, 'That's a really good score; you must be smart at this', or praised the effort made to achieve the result with a comment such as, 'That's a really good score; you must have tried really hard', or used neutral praise such as, 'That's a really good score'. Over time the students who were allocated to the effort group showed an enhancement in performance in comparison to both the control group and the trait praise group. The difference suggests that students can learn that with focus on the right things and a determined effort they can indeed improve.

This has implications as to how a manager should ideally give feedback to the trainee practising new behaviours. They should focus not on praising some underlying unobservable trait that is responsible for their job performance, but instead focus on the specific behaviours and effort that led to a successful outcome. This requires quite a shift in the way many managers think about how feedback should be provided. When Homer Simpson spoke to his children, Lisa and Bart, about a scheme of theirs that did not work, he said 'You tried your best and you failed miserably. The lesson is, never try!' Of course, you would never say something like that, but it is a wonderful example of a pure fixed mindset response to failure. Mindset also has implications on how the trainee might be coached on their self-talk about their abilities as they practice new skills. If they catch themselves denigrating their abilities with their inner dialogue after making a mistake, they should be encouraged to turn that around, so their self-talk is focused on acting differently and putting in the effort needed to overcome the difficulty.

The key to success in learning transfer is triggering new behaviours, and clearly mindset has a big part to play on whether the trigger is successful or not and how trainees react to the results and feedback they get from their efforts. Another factor is how closely the requested new behaviour resembles what was taught in the training room.

Near and far transfer

An individual understands a concept, skill, theory, or domain of knowledge to the extent that he or she can apply it appropriately in a new situation.

Howard Gardner[9]

The concept of near and far transfer of learning has been with us for more than a hundred years and is still widely discussed in the literature. The Near/Far model is probably the most commonly known of over 20 learning transfer models that have been proposed in what has become a field of study within learning theory. Many of these transfer models are based on the work done by Edward Thorndike (1874 – 1949) over 100 years ago. In a seminal article, Thorndike and Woodworth (1901) proposed their common-elements theory, according to which transfer is a function of the extent to which two domains share common features. Their theory of transfer states that the extent to which information learned in one situation will transfer to another situation is determined by the similarity between the two situations. The more similar the situations are, the greater the amount of information that will transfer. Similarly, if the situations have nothing in common, information learned in one situation will not be of any value in the other situation. In effect, the theory predicts that while near transfer takes place often, far transfer is much less common.

---

[9] From Howard Gardner's 1999 book, *The Disciplined Mind: What All Students Should Understand*

In many respects, transfer is the most critical concept in teaching. However effective instruction might otherwise be, if a learned behaviour or skill does not transfer to relevant functional application contexts and/or is not maintained over time, then the instruction has failed. Skill decay is a major problem in training. Winfred Arthur[10] and his colleagues did a metanalysis of skill decay studies and reported that the day after training, trainees exhibit little to no skill decay, but one year after training, trainees have lost over 90% of what they learned. There is greater decay for cognitive versus physical tasks, but, most importantly, Arthur et al. also reported that overall retention decreases dramatically with longer periods without practice or use of the skill.

Understanding the nuances of transfer gives us a head start in designing our training to achieve it. In the Near/Far model, near transfer occurs when the training context and trained behaviour are almost identical to the application context and application behaviour. A common example used is that of tying shoelaces. Once we have learned to tie a shoelace, it is highly likely that the skill generalises to tying all shoelaces, regardless of the length or colour or thickness of the lace or the design of the shoe. Near transfer involves the study of a problem or task and then practising it to a high level of automation. When a nearly similar problem or task is encountered, it is automatically solved or accomplished with little or no conscious thought.

This ability to generalise a skill to solve nearly similar problems has been, and still is, crucial to our species for survival. It is hard wired into us. If we didn't have it, we would have to 'learn' all over again how to tie a shoelace every time we bought a new pair of shoes. We would have to 'learn' to use a tap every time we were confronted with a tap with a new design. We would have to 'learn' to open a door every time we encountered a different design of door. And this brings us to the idea that sometimes the application context and application behaviour is sufficiently different for near transfer not to work. Imagine every tap you have seen and used has a knob to turn, and then you encounter for the first time a tap with a push button. What do you do? Imagine every door has a lever handle or a knob to turn, and you encounter a door with neither. Instead it has a push button on the wall beside the door. What do you do? We must learn to expand our skill to include a wider range

---

[10] Arther, Bennett, Stanush, and McNelly reported in *Human Performance*, (11, 57–101, 1998) on 'Factors that influence skill decay and retention: A quantitative review and analysis'

of contexts, and in doing so, create some higher-level ideas in our mind that will enable us to solve problems that are even further away from what we first learned. Now we are transferring concepts to guide problem solution rather than directly applying automated routines. This is called far transfer. Far transfer tasks involve skills and knowledge being applied in situations that change, where the application of the skill is executed differently depending on the situation. In far transfer, the learner adapts their actions, based on their judgement of the situation.

It is important to realise that near and far transfer occur on a continuum and the transfer is either nearer or father away from the training context and behaviour. It is also important to realise that people vary considerably in their abilities to see, feel or sense similarities between different problem situations. In any problem-solving situation, some people seem to be innately much better at far transfer than are others. Or rather, they see the similarities more easily, and thus for them it is nearer transfer, and comes more easily.

The difficulty with the theory of near and far transfer is that it does not provide a foundation or a plan for helping a person to become better at far transfer when dealing with novel and complex problems. And it does not tell us how to teach to increase far transfer. Then, in 1992, David Perkins and Gavriel Salomon published their Low Road and High Road Transfer of Learning Theory on the mechanisms of transfer.

Low road transfer happens when stimulus conditions in the transfer context are sufficiently like those in a prior context of learning to trigger well-developed semi-automatic responses. A relatively reflexive process, low road transfer figures most often in near transfer. High road transfer, in contrast, depends on mindful abstraction from the context of learning or application and a deliberate search for connections. What is the general pattern? What is needed? What principles might apply? What is known that might help? Such transfer is not, in general, reflexive or automatic. It demands time for exploration and the investment of mental effort.

The ideas encompassed in the concept of low/high road transfer start to show us how we need to teach to achieve transfer, particularly the more difficult far transfer. We all make use of strategies as we attempt to solve problems and accomplish tasks. The research literature on problem solving indicates that most people have a relatively limited repertoire of problem-solving strategies and that it is helpful to increase that repertoire. Teaching techniques for high road transfer of learning can help trainees to increase their repertoire. However, there is more to problem solving than a toolbox of strategies. Improving problem solving in a specific domain requires increasing knowledge that is specific to that domain. The learner must consciously practise utilising those new strategies in conjunction with their domain knowledge with a large range of problems and over a long period of time. Far transfer requires effort and practice, and the farther the transfer, the greater the effort required.

In today's world, employees need to solve problems and make decisions in an ever changing and complex environment. Far transfer focuses on trainees learning general concepts that may be applied in a wider set of contexts than those represented in the training setting. This is not to say that you should never train for near transfer. For example, there is little room for error when training someone to safely operate a power tool. Here, a near transfer training approach is more appropriate, so trainees can replicate the training behaviour as closely as possible.

We can sit here nodding and say that these transfer theories make a kind of sense, but then what? How does an understanding of these theories affect how we should design and train?

If we accept that near transfer is easier to accomplish and more likely to happen, then where we can, we should train so that the required transfer to get the desired performance improvement is as 'near' as possible. In other words, we should design training that simulates or mimics the working environment and then teach procedures. Think of this as teaching 'how' to do something and developing routine expertise. Stop for a moment and remember when you learned 'how' to do things, such as drive a car, ride a bike, handle a power tool, swim or use a computer. Remember the process you went through, and where you did it, so that these skills are now largely reflexive responses to any situation that requires them. As you practised your new skill, repeated the new behaviours and refined your learning, you became consciously competent and eventually unconsciously competent.

Although few of us have done this, imagine the process that an airline pilot goes through to learn their skills and how their training programmes make extensive use of tools such as flight simulators. You might have encountered learning in a simulated environment if you have practised various tasks using a software system in a test environment or even doing something as simple as practising a mail merge task with test data before doing it with real data. The skills gained from practice opportunities during a training programme are more likely to transfer well into the work environment when they fit without reworking or modification. Building this training and practice environment to mimic the real world is obvious in principle, but often programme designers and trainers don't have a sufficiently profound understanding of the environment where the learner will use their new skills. It's therefore necessary to collaborate with both the organisation and the participants to build relevant practice into the programme. Too often, this research into the learners' work environment is not done, and the resulting learning transfer is poor because the classroom instruction is too 'far' away from the learners' working reality. Another problem occurs when a training course, once developed, is rolled out to users who are in a different work environment, perhaps in a different country or factory, or when the course is continued although changes in the work environment have made it much less relevant and therefore less effective.

There are many things you can do in the classroom to create real-life scenarios. You can set the 'classroom' up to be the same as a house to practise installing wiring or plumbing; you can use role-plays and actors, or you can immerse trainees in solving realistic problems that they will face back in the workplace. You can introduce digital solutions, such as videos, with branching right through to simulators and the virtual reality tools that do an amazing job of recreating the real working environment. In the training centre of a big furniture retailer I visited, they had built part of a house that included stairs with an awkward corner, and delivery trainees would practise carrying a new bed up the stairs without damaging the wallpaper. The ultimate practice environment, of course, would be the Star Trek holodeck, where the learner would be in a totally safe yet totally real scenario, in which they could practise, experiment and learn. But it's going to take a while before Star Trek technology is available to L&D; indeed most L&D budgets cannot even stretch to many of today's simulation tools, although virtual reality programmes are looking promising.

Wait a minute! Haven't we already got something close to holodeck technology? It's called real-life! Within the real-life context of the workflow we can set up scenarios and, with appropriate risk management, we can get the learner to practise, experiment and learn, just where they will be required to use their skills for real. Unless we consider the inevitable complexities of the real world, the instruction we design is likely to be far too simplistic for transfer to occur to the degree needed. Sometimes we trainers forget that we can 'extend' our programme well beyond the classroom or formal event and into real life, providing varied practice in a range of contexts. How can you use the real-life 'holodeck' that is available to you? On-the-job training has grown in popularity because of the frequency with which out-of-context training fails to transfer to on-the-job performance. This is another way to reduce transfer distance, because we are using the holodeck of on-the-job context. Within that context, as trainees begin to master a skill, the training and practice conditions should be increasingly difficult; there should be less and less trainer support, and practice conditions should increasingly resemble transfer conditions. Practice opportunities should require trainees to engage in the same cognitive processes they will need to use when they graduate from practice to work.

As you look at practice scenarios, you will notice that most require trainees to use judgment in addition to, or instead of, a reflexive response. We are running into the need for high road transfer, where we need to teach more than just 'how'. We need to also teach 'why'. We need to teach adaptive expertise and creativity. You could think of this as another higher layer of learning, one that is required above the mechanistic and reflexive response. In reality, the two are on a continuum and cannot be readily separated. Given your desired outcomes for the programme, where on this continuum do your transfer needs fall?

One of the things that happens in real life is that we encounter problems that are in some way new to us. So one thing you can do in your quest to mimic reality is to give people problems to solve before you have trained them how to solve those problems. Give them access to the resources they would have in the real world; in other words, make it real. Provided you ensure that there is sufficient corrective feedback in place, you will find that the learning is often better retained and transfers better to the real world. In addition, as people tackle varying problem scenarios, they will start to develop their own approach and process for solving problems. In many ways, this is what lies at the heart of high road transfer. Solving a problem, with or without support, is always going to be a better training solution than spoon-feeding people information and theory that they then must translate into, and somehow use, in a problem situation they later encounter at work. EM Forster said it best, "Spoon feeding in the long run teaches us nothing but the shape of the spoon". There is an old saying that in theory, theory works in practice, but in practice, theory never quite works as theory predicts. It reminds me that the military have a saying that no battle plan survives first contact with the enemy.

Some people might say that putting people into a problem scenario without first doing some spoon-feeding will mean that they make mistakes, and it is the mistakes they will remember. This would be the case if you didn't give them sufficient and supportive corrective feedback and ensure they go through the scenario again and again to practise success. Some difficulty, as opposed to making it too easy to get to a solution, will enhance learning and retention and may also improve motivation to learn in order to solve the problem. Giving people problems to solve may also bring up an interesting situation, in which the trainee is confident at first glance they can solve the problem, but then finds that they can't. This can happen because they are relying on incorrect information, perhaps because it's out of date or is incomplete in a way that is now a critical barrier to their success.

An interesting aspect of transfer is that it can be positive or negative. In positive transfer, previous learning facilitates performance and the transfer task, whereas in negative transfer the opposite is the case: previous learning interferes with the transfer task. We are all aware that sometimes we must unlearn things so we can learn new things. In the words of Chester Barnard, "It is what we think we know that keeps us from learning." Think of the difficulties we have when we first drive in a foreign country on the opposite side of the road to the one we are used to.

It is also possible for the method of instruction to create negative transfer or barriers to transfer. This happens when trainers fail to realise the importance of task variation within the classroom. Practising with a single or very limited range of scenarios can encourage a singular response to other scenarios where that response may be inappropriate. Practising on a wider variety of tasks helps the learners to become accustomed to using their newly-acquired knowledge and skills in different situations and helps them learn that they will encounter different but similar situations, thus encouraging transfer of learning to the job. In effect, encourage transfer of learning from one practise scenario to another as much as you can, both in the classroom and with activities following the training, so the act of learning transfer itself is learned.

Creating new habits

We are what we repeatedly do. Excellence, then, is not an act, but a habit.

Will Durant[11]

Usually, when we talk about learning transfer, our desired outcome is that after employees learn something they will utilise that learning to behave differently, not once, but many times. Doing something a significant number of times means we enter the realm of habits. So, let's look at habits to help us understand how they can both help and hinder us in our quest for learning transfer.

A simple definition of a habit is that it is something we do often and regularly, perhaps without even being aware of the fact that we are doing it. Habits have a sense of the automatic about them and as a result they are difficult to stop or give up. In our day-to-day lives we are acutely aware of habits and how they impact on us either getting or not getting what we want in life. This has spawned a huge branch of the self-help and personal development industry; if you do a search for 'habits' on Amazon, you get over 20,000 results in the books section.

Our brains are fundamentally lazy, or efficient depending on your point of view, and create automated pathways by wiring together thoughts, emotions

---

[11] Although often attributed to Aristotle, Will Durant coined this phrase to summarise some ideas from Aristotle's writings in his book the Story of Philosophy (1926)

and behaviours so these can then be run on autopilot. These automated habit pathways come online and offline throughout the day in response to situational triggers, usually with little conscious awareness. If we are aware of them, we tend to classify habits as good or bad, depending on whether we consider them beneficial to us or not, but most habits are neutral. They are called into play as we go through our morning ritual, as we leave the house for work, as we seek out a car parking space and as we travel the same route through the supermarket aisles each time we go shopping.

All habits have some basic similarities:
- They are created by repetition
- They are triggered in response to a cue
- They are performed automatically, often with little conscious awareness
- They are persistent and hard to not do in response to the cue.

There is an old Spanish proverb "Habits are at first cobwebs, and then they become cables."

When an activity is repeated many times, the neurons that make up the circuits in the brain that drive the activity become more strongly linked. The neurons physically change, which is referred to as brain plasticity, and the neuronal circuit for the activity becomes more stable. This effect has been popularised in the expression "Cells that fire together wire together". The concept was first introduced by Donald Hebb in his 1949 book, *The Organization of Behaviour*, and is often referred to as Hebb's rule. It is clear from this that a habit cannot form without repetition, and the more repetition there is, the more ingrained and stable in our neurology the habit becomes. It is this stability that makes a habit so useful when it is a 'good' habit, and so destructive when it is a 'bad' habit.

On the face of it, creating a new habit seems simple enough and the self-help literature would have us believe this is so. To create the new habit, decide on the situation or cue you want to use as the trigger, and then discipline yourself to do the new behaviour many, many times in response to the cue. Jim Rohn, a renowned motivational speaker said, "Repetition is the mother of skill." The complication, however, is that most things that we do during our day are habitual, so it would be very rare for us to be in a situation where we are creating a new habit that has no conflict with an existing one. According to CEOS Theory, the conflict that arises when we try to create a new habit is between the two overarching systems within the brain that control behaviour: Executive and Operational. CEOS is an acronym for Context, Executive and Operational Systems and the theory seeks to explain the limits of rational choice on behaviour modification.

The Executive System controls behaviours such as planning, reasoning, problem solving, making judgments and weighing alternatives, all of which require conscious thought and cognitive control. It is top-down in operation and requires internal dialogue and therefore language. The Operational System operates at an unconscious level to manage activities, such as walking and talking, that allow us to go about our day without having to think about them unduly. It is bottom-up in operation and is reflexive and automatic in a way that does not require language. These two systems operate together to produce our behaviour, but when we seek to introduce behavioural change, especially changes to habituated behaviour, it introduces conflict between these two systems. Changing a habit requires the executive system to override the operational system over extended periods of time and many repetitions, and this in turn requires extended and high levels of effort and attention. The ongoing conflict and dissonance generate negative emotional responses: it just doesn't feel good. Changing a habit is 'expensive' and retaining an old habit is 'cheap' in terms of both cognitive and emotional load.

The idea of there being two quite different processes guiding human behaviour is not new. The Buddha used the metaphor of the rider on the elephant. The rider is the Executive System and it can't force the elephant to do what the rider wants. The rider needs to create conditions, through training, that lead the elephant to want what its rider wants. The rider needs to be clever enough to harness and manage the power of the elephant. Another analogy is that of an organisation where the CEO is the decision maker and vison setter and requires the staff to deliver on the vision. The organisation ends up with a compromise between what the boss wants, what the staff are trained and motivated to do, and how this is constrained by the environment in which the organisation operates. In the short term, the CEO could use coercion and control to get things done their way (this is analogous to personal discipline and self-control), but in the longer term the staff need to 'own' the vision for it to come to fruition and become normal. This analogy becomes real when we think of the staff, and their predominant and recurring patterns of behaviour (the culture), as the Operational System of the organisation.

In his paper 'CEOS Theory: A Comprehensive Approach to Understanding Hard to Maintain Behaviour Change' (December 2016), Ron Borland makes these other distinctions between the two systems. The Executive System (ES) is goal-directed, whereas the Operational System (OS) is simply reacting to the environment. The ES has limited capacity and sequential processing, whereas the OS has high capacity and parallel processing. The ES only operates when invoked, which may be less than needed, whereas the OS operates at all relevant times. The ES needs to influence the OS in order to initiate behaviour, whereas the OS can generate behaviour independent of the ES. The ES can handle negation and absence, whereas the OS does not. For the ES, learning tends to be rule based, whereas for the OS, learning is the result of conditioning.

These distinctions are starting to give us an insight into habitual behaviour, some of the challenges that we face in trying to change it, and what approaches we might use to change behaviour successfully. For example, the concept of negation is interesting and forms the basis of the prevention paradox. It is not possible to obey the instruction 'Don't think of a pink elephant.' You need to generate the idea of a pink elephant before the ES can apply the negation. This carries over into instructions for behaviour, such as 'Don't spill your drink', and statements, such as 'Not smoking is good', which would initially elicit associations between 'smoking' and 'good' before the negation is applied. This explains why it is so hard to educate for prevention. To maximise congruence between conceptual meaning and OS reactions, communications should be conceptually simple and avoid negations; so instead of 'Not smoking is good', use the statement 'smoking is bad'. By conceptually simple, I mean the target audience should find it easy to relate to. For example, rather than using percentages or other abstract figures, use phrases like 'The wasted paper stacked up is higher than three double decker buses', or 'The savings we make with this new method will mean we can treat five extra patients.'

Our feelings and emotions also impact our ability to create or change habits. Negative emotion is a signal that something is wrong and therefore remedial action is required to fix the situation and avoid the negative emotion. Positive emotions, on the other hand, indicate there is no reason for concern and the current situation can be allowed to continue. What this means is that there is little incentive for us to pursue effortful behaviours, such as the effort of the ES overriding the OS to repeat a new desired behaviour, when we are already feeling good. Unfortunately, there is no negative emotional signal to us when we relapse and repeat the old, undesired behaviour. All we can do, after the fact, is berate ourselves for our lack of self-discipline and accepting the short-term reward of doing what we used to do. The difficulty of giving up an undesirable but attractive behavioural habit is typically the greatest barrier to change, and thus to achievability. Achievability can sometimes be at least partly conceived of as overcoming the desirability of the problematic behaviour. How can you reframe the old habit so that it is not so attractive in the moment?

One way is to plug into our greater desire to avoid loss rather than achieve gain. Telling people what they will lose by continuing an existing behaviour is a more powerful way to offset the comforting continuance of that behaviour than trying to educate them on what they will gain by switching behaviours. Again, this information should be relatable to the target audience, so it should be conceptually simple information that is relevant to and resonates with people like them. This means that you need to get clear on the target audience. How would they define themselves; what group would they consider themselves part of, and what matters to them? If you are profiling MS Excel users, are they occasional users, or everyday users? If you are seeking behaviours that save energy, does frugality or saving the planet drive them? Notice that we are now talking like a marketeer, so get help from your marketing buddies with this stuff.

Borland's paper divides the process of behaviour change into the following four overlapping phases.
   (1) Problem diagnosis, when the person needs to have enough information and feedback to analyse the situation and conclude that they have a problem that requires behavioural change.
   (2) Goal setting, when a decision needs to be made on what to do about the situation and what success would look like. Inevitably, there will be a balancing act when it comes to deciding what seems realistic.
   (3) Taking action, which requires an action script to describe the routine, and the cue or trigger for the new behaviour. It should also include rehearsing the stories and rationalisations that justify the effort.
   (4) Maintaining change: keeping at it requires another script to track and nudge the new behaviours into everyday use. This stage should also include a reorientation of self-image to that of someone who always does the new behaviour automatically, so the requirement

for vigilance and self-discipline can be reduced. Notice that this shift in attitude comes with the last step, and not earlier. Attitudes follow behaviour, not the other way around. You can take action with self-discipline, even when your attitude does not support the action. With time, you come to think of yourself as someone who always takes that action; that is, your attitude re-orients to the new behaviour. Therefore, when encouraging change, set behavioural expectations rather than attitudinal ones.

In addition, progress can be evaluated at any point, which, if progress has been unsatisfactory, can result in rethinking the goal to bring it into the realm of the realistic. One of the common evaluation methods used in apps to help people create habits is the 'streak'. Once the activity frequency is decided – for example, once a day, or three times a week – a streak is an unbroken chain of successfully doing the activities at the required frequency. Our natural inclination, once a short chain has been established, is to not break the chain. In effect, creating and maintaining the chain becomes a habit. It is one way the rider can work with the natural tendencies of the elephant.

Some commentators say that you can't actually break a habit, but you can mask it by attaching a different routine to the same trigger to give an equivalent or better reward, and then doing that routine over and over again until it becomes automatic. Neuroscientists have even mapped this process using brain scans. It starts in the decision-making areas of the brain – the prefrontal cortex and hippocampus. Over time, as the behaviour is repeated, the activation shifts more to the basal ganglia areas because the subjects are no longer thinking actively, they are responding automatically. And of course, this raises the inevitable question, how much time does it take to form a new habit?

Dr Maxwell Maltz, a plastic surgeon in the 1950s, noticed a pattern amongst his patients. He found that it would take patients around 21 days to become accustomed to seeing the results of the surgery. He looked at his own experience of his adjustment period to changes and found a similar pattern. He wrote "These, and many other commonly observed phenomena, tend to show that it requires a minimum of about 21 days for an old image to dissolve and a new one to gel". In 1960, Maltz published a book on his thoughts on behaviour change, including this quote. The book, *Psycho-Cybernetics*, went on to sell 30 million copies, and greatly influenced the self-help and personal success movement. The quote was shortened to the pithy "It takes 21 days to form a habit", and it lodged in popular perception. It's a shame this isn't true.

A research article by Pillippa Lally published in the *European Journal of Social Psychology* in July 2009 looked at the process of habit formation in everyday life. A total of 96 volunteers chose an eating, drinking or activity behaviour to carry out daily in the same context – for example, after breakfast – for 12 weeks. Most of the volunteers provided sufficient data for analysis to look at increases in automaticity over the study period and make projections on likely outcomes beyond the study period. The time it took participants to reach 95% of their asymptote of automaticity ranged from 18 to 254 days, with an average of 66 days. One bit of good news from the study is that missing one opportunity to perform the behaviour did not materially affect the overall habit formation process.

Support

Before you are a leader, success is all about growing yourself. When you become a leader, success is all about growing others.

Jack Welch

Given what you have read in the book so far, you are probably thinking that creating habitual behaviour change so it continues over the long term following a training course is difficult to do. And you are right; it is difficult to do. And that, of course, begs the question, 'Who is doing it?' If we want it to happen, who do we need to help? Ultimately, the person doing learning transfer is the course trainee, and if they are going to succeed at this difficult task of behaviour change, they need support. Without enough of the right kind of support, they will mostly fail to transfer and implement their new learning, and the training course is therefore mostly wasted. Mostly wasted training courses means mostly wasted training budget. If we want to avoid that wasted budget, we must support the trainee through the entire programme.

There is a commonly held myth that limits us, which is that our success is due to our individual skills, attributes and knowledge. This is especially true for those with a fixed mindset, if we relate this to Carol Dweck's model. We are taught this lesson in our formative years by the education system, and often by well-meaning parents. We are judged on what we can do as individuals, and on how we compare with others. But our real potential lies in what we can do together and what we can do when supported by the people and the ecosystem around us.

So what sort of support is needed for the trainee, and where should it come from? There is obviously direct support, perhaps from their manager, to help prepare the trainee for the programme and then help them stay focused and motivated while they implement change. There is the indirect support from the way the programme is structured and designed so it has relevant content and structured opportunities to experiment and practise. And then there is support from the organisation and the environment, including colleagues, that surrounds the trainee as they are putting learning into practice. Together, they all form a scaffold within which the trainee can build their behaviour change out of the learning from the training course. If parts of the scaffold are missing, it becomes much harder for the trainee to achieve the change.

When thinking about how to provide the supporting scaffold for learning transfer, it is important to realise that the phrase 'learning transfer' is a nominalisation. In fact, it's two of them together. A nominalisation is a noun that is generated from a verb and hides the real action because it becomes a concept rather than an action. Linguistically, it seduces us into thinking of learning transfer as a thing that exists (or doesn't) as an abstract and passive idea, rather than the sequential actions of 'learn' and 'transfer'. Learning transfer is definitely not passive. It requires action, and lots of it, on an ongoing basis, from the course trainee and many others, and it requires ongoing commitment.

Whenever I run workshops on learning transfer, I tell people their biggest challenge is going to be… you guessed it, learning transfer! I am continually amazed at how many L&D professionals think that because they have attended a workshop and know a bit more about the subject, learning transfer will somehow magically start happening. They still see, perhaps at an unconscious level, a training course or workshop as a self-contained event that provides a complete solution. You will have the same challenge with this book. How are you going to set up a support structure for yourself so that you can implement at least some of the ideas you are learning about? Learning transfer is much more than just knowledge acquisition, and it is much more than just reading this and other books on the subject.

One of the things that seems to stop people designing and delivering their programmes with an emphasis on supporting the trainee to achieve learning transfer is that they don't know where to start. Out of all the things they could be doing, they don't know which ones are important and will have the most impact. Luckily, there is a considerable body of research that can point us in the right direction. One person who has investigated all the studies, papers and academic articles on learning transfer is Dr Ina Weinbauer-Heidel.

I interviewed Dr Weinbauer-Heidel in April 2018 and this is her story. Eight years earlier, she was designing successful senior leadership programmes for a business school in Austria, and at that time her definition of success was that the courses were well subscribed and generated repeat business. Everything was going well, and then she read a book called *Die Weiterbildungslüge*, by Dr Richard Gris. The book caused quite a stir in the German speaking L&D world as it challenged the status quo with a title that translates roughly as *The Continuing Education Lie*. Dr Weinbauer-Heidel said her first reaction was denial: "How can that book be right when what I am doing here at the business school is successful?", but the idea of the systemic failure of training to generate acceptable business impact wouldn't go away. Her response was to look at the research and she was surprised to discover that there was so much of it, and that it stretched back over 110 years. Also, despite so much published information, what it didn't seem to have was any unifying or practical solution that would solve the learning transfer issue she now knew existed. At the time she was looking for a project for her PhD and chose to review the literature and find the 'holy grail', the 'secret' of learning transfer.

Her research over several years identified more than 100 determinants of transfer, and so her project changed from finding the 'holy grail', which seemed characteristically elusive, to finding a way to simplify what she had found and make it practical and useable. The simplification process focused on three main areas. One was to remove from the list the transfer determinants that were only mentioned in one study. Another was to remove those that had a low level of correlation with transfer; in other words, they were a factor, but not a significant one. The third was to remove those determinants that could not be controlled or utilised. An example of these is the intelligence of the trainee. The higher the trainee IQ, the more learning transfer occurred, but testing for intelligence before allowing someone onto a training course has some ethical and practical considerations.

She ended up with a list of 12 determinants of learning transfer that are controllable and have a high impact on transfer. She called these the '12 Levers of Transfer Effectiveness', and they give you a roadmap to follow when deciding what support will be required to succeed at enabling learning transfer. She divided these into the three areas, which have become a de facto standard following the paper *Transfer of Training: A Review and Directions for Future Research,* published by Baldwin and Ford in 1988. The areas are training design, trainee and work environment.

She published her findings and recommendations in a book *Was Trainings wirklich wirksam macht: 12 Stellhebel der Transferwirksamkeit* in December 2016. The book was translated into English in 2018 and is titled *What Makes Training Really Work: 12 Levers of Transfer Effectiveness.*

Dr Weinbauer-Heidel has kindly allowed me to reproduce her summary of the 12 Levers of Transfer Effectiveness here. I would highly recommend her book as companion reading to this one.

THE 12 LEVERS OF TRANSFER EFFECTIVENESS
Dr. Ina Weinbauer-Heidel is CEO of the Institute of Transfer Effectiveness and developer of the 12 Levers of Transfer Effectiveness
www.transfereffectiveness.com

Levers for Trainees
1. Transfer Motivation – Yes, I want it!

Trainees say	"Yes, I want this!"
Definition	Transfer motivation is defined as the desire to implement what has been learned.
Guiding question	How can you ensure that trainees have a strong desire to put into practice what they have learned?

2. Self-Efficacy – Yes, I Can!

Trainees say	"Yes, I can!"
Definition	Self-efficacy describes the extent to which someone is convinced he or she can master acquired skills in practice.
Guiding question	How can you ensure that, after a training, participants will believe in their ability to apply and master the skills they have acquired?

3. Transfer Volition – Achieving Transfer Success with Willpower

Trainees say	"Yes, I'll stay on the ball and follow through!"
Definition	Transfer volition is trainees' ability and willingness to dedicate their attention and energy to the implementation of the transfer plan, even when there are obstacles and difficulties.
Guiding question	How can you help trainees to develop the ability and willingness to persistently work on implementing their transfer plan?

Levers for Training Design

4. Clarity of Expectations – Making Goals Transparent

Trainees say	"I know what I'm supposed to learn, and I want to learn it!"
Definition	Clarity of expectations is the extent to which trainees already know, before the training, what they can expect before, during, and after the training.
Guiding question	How can you make sure that trainees know what to expect before the training and what is expected from them as a result of the training?

5. Content Relevance – Learning What is Needed

Trainees say	"The content is practical and relevant to me!"
Definition	Content relevance is the extent to which trainees experience the training content as well-matched with the tasks and requirements of their work.
Guiding question	How do you ensure that trainees perceive the training content as relevant and important for their own day-to-day work?

6. Active Practice – Learning by Doing

Trainees say	"I have already experienced, practised, and tried it during training!"
Definition	Active practice in training is the extent to which training design provides opportunities to experience and practise new behaviours that are desirable in the work context.
Guiding question	How can you ensure that the action that is aspired to in practice is experienced, tried out, and practised as realistically as possible during training?

7. Transfer Planning – Step by Step to Implementation Success

Trainees say	"I know what I am going to do, step by step, after training!"
Definition	Transfer planning describes the extent to which the transfer is prepared in training.
Guiding question	How can you ensure that trainees prepare in detail while still in training to implement what they learn?

Levers for the Organisation

8. Application Opportunities – Everyday Work is Full of Possibilities

Trainees say	"It's possible for me to apply what I've learned to situations in my day-to-day work."
Definition	Opportunities for application reflect the extent to which the necessary situations and resources for application are available in the workplace.
Guiding question	How can you ensure that participants have the opportunity, permission and assignment, plus the necessary resources to apply what they have learned?

9. Personal Transfer Capacity – We (Don't) Have the Time

Trainees say	"My working day allows me to take time to apply what I have learned."
Definition	Personal transfer capacity is the extent to which trainees have the capacity – in terms of time and workload – to successfully apply newly-learned skills.
Guiding question	How can you help ensure that trainees have enough time and capacity to apply what they have learned to their daily work?

10. Support from Supervisor – the Boss and Transfer Success

Trainees say	"My supervisor demands and encourages implementation."
Definition	Supervisor support is the extent to which trainees' supervisors actively demand, monitor, support and reinforce transfer.
Guiding question	How can you ensure that supervisors support, promote and demand the application of what trainees have learned?

11. Support from Peers – Other People's Influence

Trainees say	"My colleagues are backing me on implementing what I have learned."
Definition	Support from peers is the extent to which colleagues help trainees with transfer.
Guiding question	What can you do to encourage trainees' colleagues to welcome transfer and support it?

12. Transfer Expectations in the Organisation – Transfer Results as a New Finish Line

Trainees say	"People in the organisation notice when I (don't) apply what I have learned."

Definition	Transfer expectations in the organisation are the extent to which trainees expect positive consequences from applying what they've learned or the absence of negative consequences as a result of non-application.
Guiding question	How can you ensure that trainees' application (or not) of what they've learned is urgent, attracts attention in the organisation and has positive (or negative) consequences?

© Dr Ina Weinbauer-Heidel, 2018
Contact: ina.weinbauer-heidel@learning-transfer-at-work.com

Learning transfer is a complex system and Dr Weinbauer-Heidel's work distilling the research has helped us identify the significant levers in the system that we can pull to affect the system. As she says, "The model helps us know where to shine the flashlight". When you are convincing others of the best place to shine the flashlight, they may require evidence rather than an appeal to their common sense. Dr Weinbauer-Heidel's book is a rich source of academic papers and articles that will help you make your case for supporting learning transfer.

It's clear that providing a support scaffold using all 12 significant levers of learning transfer is not a trivial operation and involves more than just the learner and the course facilitator. Dr Weinbauer-Heidel's book focuses on what the facilitator can do and who they can directly influence to contribute to supporting learning transfer. It is a huge toolkit with which every course facilitator should become familiar. It has examples and checklists and a step-by-step approach, and I highly recommend it.

As well as implementing the 12 levers at the facilitator level, I think they can also be implemented at another level that is more strategic, and that means getting those senior people involved who are not normally within the sphere of influence of the facilitator. You need to be able to connect the senior team's desire for effective execution of the corporate strategy with the fact that employees need to achieve learning transfer to make that execution possible. The vision of what the company can become, and the strategy to achieve it, will require employees to learn both formally and informally, and grow into people who can deliver that vision. If training is part of the learning required, and it's highly probable that it is, then without adequate learning transfer following the training, the strategy will not succeed, and the vision becomes just another dream of things that might have been. No executive wants that on their resume!

The senior team has an influence on the wider organisational culture that is unavailable to the course facilitator. The cultural environment is the context within which learning transfer takes place; the friendlier the culture is to learning transfer, the easier it will be to provide support for it. Another way to think of this is to use our scaffold metaphor. The cultural environment is the foundation on which we base our scaffold; if the foundation is insecure, it will limit the scaffold we can provide. In fact, some cultures are so unfriendly to learning transfer that we could say the foundations for any scaffold we erect are in a swamp, and our attempts to provide a scaffold will be ineffective. If the cultural environment is so inimical to learning transfer, how do we convince the senior team to drain the swamp?

Large-scale cultural change is beyond the scope of this book, but the 12 levers give you a way to define some aspects of the culture that would need to change to support learning transfer. Consider each of the levers in turn, starting with the ones related to your organisation, and look at how the current culture encourages or inhibits the use of that lever, and how you would like the culture to change so the lever is easy to apply. In effect, you are starting to create your own vision of a culture that totally supports learning transfer.

When you talk to the senior team about this they will want data that support your position and explains why you want the changes. You can get what you need from the Towards Maturity reports (www.towardsmaturity.org) and in particular the report *The Transformation Curve*, published in January 2018. It is free to download from their website. Donald H Taylor writes in the report introduction… "Towards Maturity have created something which I believe will be invaluable to the L&D profession – a model of maturity that relates not only to the use of technology but to everything that L&D departments do on the road from being fulfilment houses of formal training to catalysts supporting an effective organisation. Individuals, as well as organisations, will recognise themselves in the pages of this report. Each one of the four stages described is a recognisable manifestation of how learning and development is approached today – from small to large organisations around the globe. The power of the research is to describe in six dimensions exactly what the stages look like and how to progress through them."

The report gives you the hard data you need to open effective conversations with business leaders about the imperative to progress towards a mature learning culture. It lays out the journey in stages, with markers for each stage and details how to transition between them. This means you can assess the current stage of learning maturity of your organisation and what the benefits will be of transitioning to higher levels. According to the report, the companies with the highest learning maturity are three times more likely to achieve their business outcomes than those in the lowest quartile. The behaviours and cultural dimensions of those at the top end are exactly what you need to provide a sound foundation for learning transfer. As part of the blueprint for improving learning maturity, the report talks about the growing and changing role of L&D as an organisation grows through the four stages.

I can't do the 40-page report sufficient justice here as a summary, so download it and read it for yourself. You'll be glad you did.

Measurement

In God we trust; all others must bring data.

William Edwards Deming

To know if what we have done has been successful, we need to measure the results in comparison to what was happening before. We need to keep score. These data guide our decisions on how we can change what we are doing to get more of what we want. If the data you are gathering are not going to feed into any decision, either yours or someone else's, why gather it? Most would agree that data-driven decision making is far superior to other ways of making decisions; however, the key to using data to inform decision making doesn't lie just in the data. Turn the data you collect into useful information that gets translated into understanding, knowledge and insights that will generate better decisions on an ongoing and repeatable basis. Data should act as the foundation for your decision-making process, not as a substitute for your own judgement. In effect, know the difference between data-driven decisions and data-informed decisions.

Just because you can measure something, doesn't mean it is important, and you should measure it. And just because something is difficult to measure, doesn't mean that you shouldn't try. This is particularly true in L&D, because there are many things that are easy to measure that have a low or zero correlation with the eventual business impact and won't affect any future decisions. We get seduced away from measuring business impact into measuring things like short-term knowledge retention with tests, course completions, attendance records, and how good the food was at the venue. That's not to say that metrics like these are never worth measuring, but they are wholly inadequate and distracting if you are looking for data relating to learning transfer.

Brandon Hall Group's 2018 *Learning Measurement Study* found that few organisations collect metrics that help link learning to organisational and individual performance. According to David Wentworth, their Principal Learning Analyst, only about 8% of companies truly measure different types of learning with an eye on business results. He says that organisations invest huge amounts of time, money and energy into learning, yet real insight into the impact it has on the business remains elusive. Most do a good job tracking who completed which training, but that doesn't tell the whole story or help determine learning ROI. Instead of the reporting you do now, what would you like to be reporting to your executive team in two years' time? What data do they need that are genuinely useful for their decisions?

Prof. Robert O Brinkerhoff on page 87 of his book, *The Success Case Method*, says, "Performance results cannot be achieved by training alone, therefore, training should not be the object of the evaluation". He goes on to say that this is like saying the success of a marriage depends solely on the quality of the wedding ceremony. I like this metaphor. Who has ever said "That was such a brilliant wedding, the best I have ever been to, and that definitely means the marriage will be a success!" Really? Conversely, who has ever blamed a failed marriage on the poor quality of the wedding ceremony? And yet, in the learning and development world, we seem to do this all the time when we measure a training event as a way of predicting future successful performance, or we blame poor performance on poor training. For sure, there will be an 'afterglow' from a wonderful wedding, or training event, that will carry on into real life. It is a great place to start, but it's how the sentiments and promises made at the event are transferred into day-to-day life that really counts. I am sure if you were talking to someone before their wedding, they would describe the wedding as a onetime event, albeit a significant one, that takes place on their journey to 'happily ever after'.

If we want to evaluate transfer and behavioural change from training, we must evaluate the managerial and performance system, not the training. Supervising managers hold the keys to ongoing performance improvement because they are responsible for the day-to-day performance management activities that most shape behaviour. Brinkerhoff's Success Case Method (SCM) attempts to understand the success of training within the context of the whole performance environment. Training is only one input to performance improvement. In a nutshell, SCM focuses on the extremes – the successful and unsuccessful adopters – and then looks at what is working, and what isn't, and why. It posits that more useful information is gained by studying the outliers rather than the average. It's a structured after-action review that is qualitative/anecdotal, rather than data-driven, to look for ways to improve the whole process, so the organisation enhances its capability to leverage learning into business value. It is quick and simple in comparison to other, more data-driven models, which makes it more likely to be done. It is also very useful when prototyping and testing a new training programme with an agile/iterative approach.

Brinkerhoff's research came up with the figures that 15% of trainees never apply their new skills, 70% make some effort but then give up and return to old habits, and only 15% will apply them over the longer term. Does this 'feel' right to you from your experience? Can you do better than that with your training programmes, and if so, how much better? And how much better would your results need to be for them to be considered 'reasonable' by an external observer? I originally trained as a mechanical engineer and if only 15% of the machines I designed were successful, I would have had a lot of unhappy customers, and probably a few dead ones as well. If you went to the dentist and only 15% of the fillings you received stayed in place over the long term, would you be happy with that dentist? When put in those terms, the success rate of traditional training interventions is appalling, yet often people seem so reluctant to do anything to improve it.

One of the things I find fascinating when discussing learning transfer with people is their reluctance to spend money on learning transfer activities. They claim they do not have any budget available, but this is simply not true. Consider the following scenario, based on Brinkerhoff's transfer figures. A company puts 10 trainees in a training room at £100 each and, let's be generous here, 20% of them pick up the learning and transfer it into acceptable and sustained performance improvement. The company has paid £1,000 to get two people up to the required standard. Whoever has signed off that training course has agreed to pay £500 per trainee for a successful result for that trainee. If that same training course, embedded into a learning transfer programme, could even just double the number of trainees with sustained performance improvement, then surely it is worth spending double for the whole programme, right? Think about it.

Besides the Success Case Method, there are other well-known measurement models – all of which have their fans and critics. I suggest you get familiar with at least the basics of the main models. The best-known one is the Kirkpatrick Model, which you can find at www.kirkpatrickpartners.com. This model was extended by Jack Phillips and you can read more about his work at www.roiinstitute.net. It is interesting to note that both these models have been modified over the years to help people go beyond measurement and think more about programme design. In other words, rather than train and then measure, they encourage people to design an appropriate programme, working backwards from the measures they desire to achieve. Since both models involve measuring behaviour change and business results at some level, this means that they are now espousing learning transfer activities. They have both taken to heart the second habit espoused by Dr Stephen R. Covey, 'Begin with the end in mind'.

You might also be interested in some work Dr Will Thalheimer has done to create a new model that he calls 'The Learning-Transfer Evaluation Model' (LTEM)[12]. In his words, "The model, which I've named the Learning-Transfer Evaluation Model (LTEM, pronounced L-tem) is a one page, eight-level model, augmented with color coding and descriptive explanations. In addition to the model itself, I've prepared a 34-page report to describe the need for the model, the rationale for its design, and recommendations on how to use it." And, "This report introduces a serious practical alternative to the Kirkpatrick-Katzell model. The proposed new model is aligned with the science of learning and is intentionally designed to catalog a more robust set of requirements than the Kirkpatrick-Katzell model – requirements targeted to overcome the most urgent failures in learning practice. In short, the new model provides more appropriate guideposts, enabling us as learning professionals to create virtuous cycles of continuous improvement. The new model is relevant to educational contexts as well, where learning doesn't necessarily focus on job performance per se, but on other future applications of learning." The report, and the model proposed, encourage some new thinking around the way we focus on measuring learning transfer and I would recommend reading it if you are serious about measurement. It certainly gave me a lot of food for thought.

---

12 Thalheimer, W. (2018), 'The learning-transfer evaluation model: Sending messages to enable learning effectiveness.' Available at https://WorkLearning.com/Catalog

Adding measures to any training programme will add some cost in terms of time and effort, and this raises the question of who pays. Consider other purchases that an organisation might make to improve performance. The supplier of a new computer-controlled machine tool for a workshop is not called upon to justify the purchase over the longer term. It is the purchaser who, if they are so inclined, needs to look at the Return On this Investment (ROI) in comparison to keeping the old machine that was replaced. The supplier may well give some pointers on ways to measure the ROI, but they never see that measurement as their direct responsibility. It is interesting that when people 'purchase' a training course, unlike the purchaser of the machine tool, somehow they don't see themselves as responsible for measuring the ROI or often even justifying the purchase. So, who is responsible for measurement? The answer to this question is even less clear-cut when it is the internal L&D department supplying the training and the 'purchaser' is another part of the same business.

One of the first steps when designing any training programme is to figure out how you are going to measure your results, because the act of deciding on measures will make sure you get clarity on what it is you are seeking to achieve. You can come back to the measures later, after you have a more detailed programme design, and then again after running a pilot group or two, but thinking about them up front is incredibly useful. As you start the design of a training programme, you should already have the output from your performance diagnostics process that proves a training programme is part of a viable solution to the original problem. One of the steps in the diagnostics process is to define the gap between where things are now, and where they need to be. Therefore, one of the outputs of the process is a description of the current state and a 'vision' of the future desired state. One of the first things you must consider in programme design is how you are going to measure your progress across the gap towards that desired state.

Here is an interesting question to ask of yourself, and all the other stakeholders: if the training programme achieves 100% impact, what would that look like? Don't try and define for them what 100% impact means, just allow them to make assumptions and answer your question. You will be surprised at the assumptions they make and how the answers to that question will vary. Is this variability a problem? Does anyone even think 100% impact is possible? Ask them what percentage is possible and why. Ask them what is acceptable and why, and ask them what that looks like in comparison to 100% impact. Ask them what it would look like when trainees are halfway towards the outcome and how long that halfway point might take to reach. Notice there's a message in this question that presupposes this is a journey that takes time rather than a once-off event. In effect, you are talking about an estimated result and an aspirational target. Also ask them what is unacceptable and what happens if the results are below the required threshold. Then ask them how they would measure the impact if they were to do the measurement. Some of these stakeholders are going to be looking at the results you get based on what you measure, and they will judge you based on what they see. Make sure you know what they are looking for, or what success means to them. Your future depends on it. The reason I say this is because learning is essential only to the degree that it contributes more to performance than some other use of scarce resources. The fundamental promise of training is an improvement of employee performance in exchange for some of their time and some budget. If you can't keep that promise by delivering return on that investment, then what?

Here are some other questions to get you started...

- What change are you trying to drive within the business?
- What measures are already in place relating to the change?
    - What other factors do you need to measure?
    - Observable behaviour changes?
    - How do trainees feel about themselves?
    - Impact on costs or profitability from changed actions, processes etc.?
    - Engagement and satisfaction?
    - Completion rates and other direct programme stats?
    - Competency, confidence, commitment?
    - Can trainees do what they were trained to do successfully?
    - Stakeholder ratings on the programme itself?
- What measures can you design to fill in the gaps?
- How often during the programme do you need to measure?
- How can you do before and after snapshots?
- How can you prove the costs of learning transfer activity are justified?
- What are the costs of 'doing' versus 'not doing'; that is, can you run a control group?

Measures are a way of quantifying consequences, but by their very nature, they are after-the-fact. You should also seek to predict consequences with a thought experiment by asking these four questions:
1. What would happen if we did it?
2. What would happen if we didn't do it?
3. What wouldn't happen if we did it?
4. What wouldn't happen if we didn't do it?

At first glance this may seem a trivial exercise, but it will give you valuable insights and can be applied to anything you are considering doing in relation to the training programme. Given a scenario, most people struggle with one or two of these questions because it is not the way their mind naturally works. In effect, they have encountered a blind spot, and these questions are designed to help you see into the blind spot. Write down the consequences predicted within the answers to these questions, prioritise these consequences, and then consider how you could measure the high-priority consequences, perhaps both quantitatively and qualitatively.

The measures you decide to use will dictate where the data must come from and how you could gather it together. Some data will come from the business operations, because if you are not trying to move needles on the business dials, what is the training programme for? Other data will come from the training programme itself. This will be easier if you are using a digital platform for some aspects of the programme because a lot of data is captured automatically, including the results of questionnaires, access time and so on. The most common platform will be one of the myriads of Learning Management Systems (LMS), but an alternative is a Learning Transfer Platform (LTP), which is a relatively new genre of tool. I first saw an LTP described in a *Chief Learning Officer Magazine* article in February 2017, written by Robert O. Brinkerhoff. "An LTP is a cloud-based software platform that wraps custom-designed interactions and learners' engagements around and into more traditional employee development workshops and seminars. This creates a learning/performance improvement journey for each participant."

An LTP will allow you to put a wrapper around your training course to manage the entire learning journey, including all the activities focused on learning transfer. It will have reporting and alerts to hold the various stakeholders accountable, and provide ways of measuring results and change over the course of the programme. An LTP can operate standalone or alongside your LMS to manage learning transfer. From a 70:20:10 perspective, you could say it is managing the 70 and 20 parts of the learning journey, which are outside the classroom. One way I like to differentiate between an LMS and an LTP is that the LMS is focused on content delivery, whereas the LTP is focused on delivering activities. A lot springs from this subtle distinction.

I must confess to a vested interest here as my company, People Alchemy Ltd, has developed a world class Learning Transfer Platform. Brinkerhoff's article at http://www.clomedia.com/2017/02/09/37372/ does a great job of describing our LTP and some of the benefits it can provide :-)

Another technology that is gathering momentum is the Experience API, or xAPI. This is an e-learning software specification that allows different learning systems to speak to each other in a manner that records and tracks all types of learning experiences. The learning experiences are recorded in a centralised Learning Record Store (LRS), which is designed to hold huge amounts of data and make it accessible for reporting. If you are starting to think 'big data' for your learning measurement, you should be looking into xAPI. For more on xAPI, go to their website at www.xapi.com.

The measures you choose and the way you report them will impact the 'brand' of the training programme and the 'brand' of L&D, so let's look at what brand means for learning transfer.

The brand of L&D

Your brand is what other people say about you when you're not in the room.

Jeff Bezos, CEO and Founder of Amazon

Well, what do people say about L&D when you are not in the room?

Here is a thought experiment for you. On second thoughts, why don't you make it a real experiment, and do it for real? Go around and ask people in your organisation, particularly managers at all levels, what they think about Learning & Development.

- What do they think is the purpose of L&D?
- What do they think L&D does?
- What value do they think L&D adds to the organisation?
- Who do they think L&D really is?
- What touch points do they have with L&D?
- Ask them what they say about L&D when you are not in the room.

This is your brand. Do you like it? Does this brand work for you? Does this brand allow you to operate effectively within the organisation? Most people I speak with say the answer is 'no'. Their current brand limits their ability to be effective in the way they would like. I saw this comment from Josh Bersin of Bersin by Deloitte, "Our newest research (High-Impact Learning Organization 2017) shows that employees we surveyed rate the L&D department a -8 Net Promoter score (extremely low). I suggest this score is lower than most of us would even rate the IRS." One of the reasons that the brand is so poor in organisations is that people have the impression that training does not make that much difference, and the reason for this is insufficient learning transfer.

Your training programme is an entity that has its own brand. At a simplistic level, people may say "It's a good course", or "Don't bother, it's not worth the time" or their reaction to the brand may be much more nuanced. This brand has developed because of the accumulated experiences people have when they interact with the programme at the touch points. Whenever there is a touch point, an impression is formed by the 'touchee' and gets added to the brand they have developed in their mind. Many of those touch points are under your control, but some of them are not, because they are one step removed. For example, if two people are talking in the cafeteria about your programme, that is a touch point for them – even though you are unaware of it. Are those people recommending your programme or dissing it?

If the brand of a training programme is poor, trainees will be reluctant to go on the programme and managers will be reluctant to release them. Why would they, if everybody 'knows' the programme is not good? If that programme is mandatory, how likely are they to support learning transfer after the workshop with the bad reputation? If your training programme has a good brand, people will give it the benefit of the doubt. However, if the brand is poor, it will carry the blame for many things that may not even have much to do with the programme itself.

For all the stakeholders you identified when you did your stakeholder analysis, consider all the touch points that will take place during the training programme and what the likely impression will be, given how those touch points will play out. Look at every touch point and consider how you could improve the experience, and therefore the brand, even by just a small amount. Also consider whether you have enough touch points, or even too many. Decide ahead of time, as part of your initial design process, what you want the brand of the training programme to be – in other words, what you want people to say about it when you are not in the room. Then proactively create a brand experience by ensuring the touch points are congruent with the desired brand.

Of course, the training programme brand will sit under the umbrella brand of L&D, and this can cast a long shadow. I talk about the brand of L&D as the fourth sneaky elephant. We have already met the first three elephants, namely learning transfer, performance diagnostics and informal learning. If these three elephants are not dealt with openly, the fourth elephant will sneak into the room. You could put together a marketing campaign to alter the brand of L&D and deal with the fourth elephant, but unless you deal with the first three elephants, particularly learning transfer, your campaign will fail.

Getting learning transfer right is one of the biggest levers that L&D has to create impact in the organisation. Successful learning transfer depends on a mindset that permeates the entire learning programme from design through delivery to the end game. It depends on a focus on business benefits rather than learning outcomes. It depends on all the stakeholders being aware of and committing to their responsibilities to the programme. It depends on those stakeholders being held accountable for their assigned activities. And it depends on sufficient measurement to provide feedback for improvement, and awareness that you have crossed the finish line and the programme has succeeded.

Part 2: The Practical Stuff

The difference between what we are doing and what we are capable of doing would solve most of the world's problems.

Mahatma Gandhi

This part of the book requires you to do a little work by wielding a high-lighter. It is an unstructured potpourri of tips, ideas and questions that focus on the practical aspects of adding learning transfer to your training programme. Every programme will be different, and probably a bit messy and iterative. Trying to force-fit it into a strait jacket will not be helpful, or indeed, even possible. What I have tried to do is pull together lots of ideas you can take and make your own. Please consider all of them. Just because it is not immediately obvious how an idea might work for you, doesn't mean it won't work. Indeed, you may need to test a few before accepting or rejecting them for your programme. Another reason for this approach is that you get more ideas and tools with less fluff than you would in a typical book. It is more efficient to use bullet points and questions without lots of text that tries to join up the dots.

Other than a nod to the likely sequence of when you might use these ideas, I have not attempted to make them 'flow' from one to another, so just dip in anywhere. Also, this section contains many contributions from L&D practi-tioners, and I thank them for sharing their thoughts and experiences for us to learn from. I wanted to collate the ideas from many people and put them together with my own to get a 'collective wisdom'. Thus, you will find overlap, and even some apparent disagreement. Please note that these contributions are not being held up as examples of best practice. They are simply stories and thoughts from the real world; from your peers who are also looking to get more from their training budget.

You will find the same idea more than once, but stated in different ways. You will find ideas where the connection with learning transfer may seem tenuous at first glance, but trust me, it has a reason for being in the book. Pick your way through all the ideas that follow; select the ones that you feel may work for you, and weave them into your own tapestry to make it brighter and better. Go back again and again, because as you implement an idea, others will make more sense and become more relevant to you.

I encourage you to scribble in the margins and use a highlighter; use sticky tabs to mark bits that resonate with you and share them with colleagues. Treat this like a workbook, not a text book that must be returned pristine to the school library. Make this book work for you, day after day. We'd love to see a photo of your well-used book. Send it in and we'll post it online :-)

Tips, ideas, tools and questions to get you thinking

1. Wisdom from Steve Jobs

"Design is a funny word. Some people think design means how it looks. But of course, if you dig deeper, it's really how it works." Steve Jobs

2. Use pixie dust (or equivalent magic)

When a manager asks for training for members of their team, you need to find out if they think you have supplies of pixie dust, or some other magical equivalent. You will know this because there is an implicit assumption in their request that people who leave your training room will be fully operational and immediately competent to perform. I am sure you can resonate with the comment someone made to me regarding a large-scale training initiative: "When they looked into the project they found that the leaders had considered that the change had been implemented once everyone who would be using the new technique had been on a training course." They believed that:

1. Exposure to content = training
2. Training = learning
3. Learning = behaviour change
4. Behaviour change = improved performance
5. Improved performance = their problem solved.

This extended equation is only true when it is sprinkled with pixie dust. Now, if you are lucky enough to have a supply and a pixie dealer on speed-dial so that you can get more, then go right ahead and use it. I envy you, and please let me know who your dealer is and where I can find him. If, like most of us, you don't have a pixie dust dealer, then you need to gently explain this to the manager. The best way to do this is to take them through a performance diagnostic process first, and then explain what will be needed for learning transfer to create operational effectiveness without using pixie dust.

3. It is not the message that matters

People in L&D, and by extension the people they serve in the organisation, often think the message/content is what counts. It's not. It's what people do with the message/content that really counts. What do you want to happen *after* they receive the message/content?

4. The words you use matter; learning versus development

I worked with a professional firm who ran an internal survey. The results were intriguing. Employees said that they received plenty of training, but not enough development. Further investigation revealed that staff felt they had access to as much training and online learning as they could wish for, but they did not get many opportunities to 'develop': to practise, to experiment, to shadow and observe experts, to do tasks that stretched them, and to reflect and collaborate with peers on their experiences. Do you want to deliver learning/training, or development?

5.   Where to focus

"You don't get results by focusing on results. You get results by focusing on the actions that produce results." Mike Hawkins.

So, work backwards from the results you want, to the actions that people need to do, to how you will enable them to take those actions.

6.   Changing culture

It is almost certain that some changes will be needed to the culture of an organisation in order to make it friendlier for learning transfer, and if the culture needs to change, each person is part of the solution or part of the problem. Some people stand higher than others; these are the people whom others see as leaders. What they do and what they say, and what they don't do and what they don't say are clues that others use as a basis for their own behaviour.

Who can help you by being part of the solution, and who might be a barrier? In the words of Gandhi, who can "Be the change you want to see in the world"?

7.   Why the manager is so key to learning transfer

No one is better positioned than the manager to
- motivate learners to engage in learning
- understand the learning needs of people on their team
- know the day-to-day life of their team members and thus know how and when learning experiences will fit and have impact
- aid in the accumulation and personalisation of learning
- be an agent of change for the learner
- be a role model
- hold the learner accountable for practising their new learning
- be accountable to the learner for providing support
- respond to and help with any stress created by the learning programme
- manage the environment around the learner to support transfer

- help the learner see the relevance of the learning
- coach and mentor through the learning transfer journey.

How can you convince the manager that it is worth their time and effort to support their team members' development?

Story: Leading leaders
Contributed by: Graham Joyce, COO at IMD Ltd

During my time working within a large US corporate, I was fortunate to have been selected for their advanced leadership programme. This was an internal training programme combining various classroom sessions, coaching, and an action learning project that stretched over a 12-18 month period. Six years later, I continue to reflect upon and leverage what I learned and experienced on the programme, the full scope of which would span many pages and chapters. These experiences cover both the good and the bad, and I have gained benefit from both.

One of the good (indeed excellent) parts of the programme came through one of the 3-day classroom sessions, titled "Leading Leaders". This was, in fact, a training module where delegates were taught the fundamentals of coaching, how to access coaching within the company, and how to become coaches ourselves. The sessions included PowerPoint, personality assessments, group discussions, workshops, and even the dreaded role play (subsequently played back to us as it had been video recorded). When the sessions ended on day three, I left with a wealth of reference material and three things of enduring value:

1. A coach. A number of the discussions and workshops were supported by senior leaders within the business.

One offered to provide coaching to the delegates on an ongoing basis, and I snapped up the offer.

2. A diary. Part of the agreement of securing my coach is that our informal yet frequent engagements would be framed around a coaching diary that I would keep. Therein I would record my attempts at coaching, with any successes, failures, and observations. More on this later.

3. A new network of colleagues from across our international business whom I had never met before, and some of whom I remain in contact with today. I did not appreciate it at the time, but these were to provide a mixture of coaches and coachees for both myself and colleagues over the coming years.

I didn't appreciate the value of the diary at first as it was originally viewed with some healthy British cynicism. I now realise, of course, that I was being moved up the 'learning stack' and received some accountability coaching. The diary forced me to reflect, firstly with myself, and then with my coach, on what I had actually experienced, and how I could improve. It also motivated me to seek out coaching and mentoring opportunities; initially to avoid embarrassing gaps in the diary, and subsequently through a desire to put identified improvements into practice.

I must be honest, as time passed, the diary, as a physical entity, went into decline. In terms of a complete historical record, this is a shame. However, the good news is that this self-reflection and reflecting with others have now become second nature to me. I still encourage others to keep diaries, be it related to coaching or any other development objective. Those that do continue keeping a diary are typically those who stick with it and show long-term, sustained development. It is certainly an excellent way to get you and your team up what I now recognise as the 'learning stack'. It is an excellent way to apply some accountability within what is typically a voluntary, background activity that requires sustained effort once the realities of the day job kick in.

© Graham Joyce, 2018
Contact: graham.joyce@learning-transfer-at-work.com

8. Managers as an extension of L&D

How can you treat the management population as collaborators in this learning transfer? Think of them as part of the L&D department rather than a separate group that needs to be coerced into action. How can you build into them the same desire for improvement in performance?

9. Adding salt to the manager's oats

Someone once said to me that the managers in their organisation just didn't want to get involved: "You can take a horse to water, but you can't make it drink." The solution to that is to add enough salt to the horse's oats so that they are thirsty enough to *want* to drink. So how can you add salt to the manager's oats?

The same thinking, but different salt, can be used for the trainees. What can you build into your programme that will make the trainees want to participate? What can you do to make the trainees want to complete, not just the classroom session, but all the follow-up activities, until they are successful in generating the desired changes? How can you salt their oats?

10. Getting managers to help trainees with learning transfer

The local line manager, and their input into the learning transfer process, are critical success factors for learning transfer. Consider how you can set things up so that the line manager wants to do this, as opposed to being forced to do it or doing nothing.

- Can they be held accountable for a measure that indicates the level of learning transfer?
- Does their job description include their role in supporting learning transfer?
- Does their manager support and promote the programme?
- Do the managers even want the programme?
- Do the managers see the learning programme as relevant?
- Were the managers involved in creating the programme?
- Do they have any sense of ownership of the programme or its content?
- Will the desired learning transfer help the managers meet their objectives?
- Do they understand their role in learning transfer?
- Do they see their learning transfer duties as an imposition or an integral part of the job?
- How are they, or could they, be rewarded for performing their learning transfer duties?
- What do the managers need to believe is true for them to participate in learning transfer?
- What do they need to believe is true for them to not wish to participate?
- How are they measured and thereby encouraged to prioritise their activities?

11. Getting stakeholders on your side

Use the idea and stats in this book to convince the stakeholders of the need to change and make a genuine effort to change from event-based training to learning programmes in a learning transfer climate. Make sure that stakeholders are aware of the typical training failure stats and use this as a backdrop for your explanation as to why this next programme will be run differently. Explain why you are doing what you are doing and enlist their help in designing the learning transfer activities.

Make trainees and managers aware of the overall costs of the programme, and what the likely benefits and returns are if it is just a training event or if it is a full learning transfer programme. If they don't step up, they are wasting a lot of company money.

12. Keep stakeholders in the loop

How can you set up appropriate communication channels for all stakeholders during the programme? Who are the stakeholders? What data do they need and when do they need it? What will they be looking for in the data? Hopefully you started the programme with clarity on what success would look like for each of them, so you can report on your progress toward the agreed goals for the programme in terms of what matters to them.

13. Who is responsible for the programme?

At an overall level, who is going to be responsible for the learning programme? Building a RACI accountability matrix is useful for learning programmes. The RACI roles are Responsible, Accountable, Consulted and Informed. The RACI model describes the participation by various roles in completing tasks or deliverables for a project or business process. It is especially useful in clarifying roles and responsibilities in cross-functional/departmental projects and processes. It is simple to use, a powerful way to keep track of the roles that different people have within a learning project, and provides a level of governance. There is plenty of information available on the internet to get you started with RACI.

14. Where is the leadership pointing?

Very few organisations are satisfied with where they are, and any leadership team worth its salt will have a vision of where they want to be instead. They will promote their vison with passion and enlist people in achieving it. If they do this well, people will want to follow; they will want to engage with the vision and be a part of the journey towards a better future.

If an employee wants to participate and contribute, they will do what they need to do to get involved. They will find out what they need to find out; they will put in the time and effort. They will learn what they need to learn so their contribution to achieving the vision can be effective and meaningful. Adults tend to be goal-oriented learners, so if they have a goal, they will learn what they need to pursue that goal. This is why leadership is so important for learning in an organisation. It's not that the leaders must espouse learning, although that is helpful. It is that they give people a yearning for better things.

The opposite is also true. If leadership is poor and there is no unifying and inspiring vision, employees accept the status quo, which in turn does not require them to stretch and learn or do anything differently.

15. What is in it for them?

Trainees are different in terms of their needs and wants. Some want security; some want growth; some want social opportunities and approval; some want certainty, and so on. So, to sell them on wanting to do the programme, you must sell it to them based on what they want rather than on what you think they should want. As best you can, put yourself in their shoes and imagine what they might want from the programme that would help them engage with it, but unless you are a master of empathy, this will only take you so far.

In the material you use to market the course, and in the briefings you give to managers to help them prepare a trainee for the course, you can add different statements that hit different motivational buttons. For example, to a trainee who wants visibility and approval you can point out how it will increase their chances for promotion and rewards; to someone who wants security, point out how it will help them retain their job in uncertain times, and to the growth-minded person, explain how it will help them reach their potential.

Story: Falling at the last hurdle
Contributed by: Mervyn Humphries

As a young, inexperienced project worker, I was asked to devise a staff evaluation process for a local council. This was seen as a very useful tool by new, progressive managers who wanted to copy best practices from other industries. It seemed an interesting new venture that might improve a wide range of work practices like supervision standards, decisions about promotion and training, etc.

I became fascinated by this project and devised an evaluation form after consultation with each of the four teams of staff who would use it. The teams were very enthusiastic about it because they saw this as quite an improvement on the old, informal methods.

They learned how judgements about performance needed to be backed up by evidence and open to challenge. Indeed, they looked forward to seeing its implementation. The senior manager involved was also delighted.

We were about to set a starting date when the manager thought he should just check if the HQ staff were also in favour. I hadn't thought about that link in the chain - I assumed that this innovation had been cleared at the start.

The message came back with two weak reasons why we could not go ahead, namely that the Unions would need to be consulted and that perhaps evaluation should apply to a wider range of staff.

These were hard lessons in how change management works and how transfers can be stopped in their tracks.
- First, other industries may well have good ideas that should be adopted. However, a range of stakeholders and decision makers need to share this view and demonstrate their commitment.
- Secondly, several obstacles often need to be overcome - this takes time, diplomacy and planning.

To fall at the first hurdle is painful; to fall at the last hurdle is not only painful but also disappointing because more time and energy will have been spent. To change established traditions takes a well-crafted strategy, even if there are strong reasons to improve them.

I left the organisation 15 years later. Staff evaluation remained exactly the same for twenty years. Learning, innovations and new methods do not transfer under their own steam.

© Mervyn Humphries, 2018
Contact: mervyn.humphries@learning-transfer-at-work.com

16. Identify limiting beliefs

Do the trainees believe they can change their behaviour? Henry Ford said, "Whether you think you can or whether you think you can't, you are right". Investigate what beliefs the trainees are likely to have about their ability to make the desired changes in behaviour after the training course.

What do they think, rightly or wrongly, will be the obstructions or barriers to change? If the barriers are real and significant, they need to be removed before it is worth running the training course. If the barriers are not real, and only imagined by the trainees, then you need to help them change those beliefs.

17. Change can be viral

One of the most significant determinants of learning transfer is the culture of the organisation; after all, this is the sea within which all other learning transfer activities swim. If you want to change the culture, Dr Leandro Herrero in his book *Viral Change* (July 2008) suggests that change happens when socially-contagious behaviours spread slowly through an organisation and reach a tipping point, after which they become the norm. He sees change as an infection that spreads and generates new ideas, processes and behaviours within the culture.

Think of culture as a collection of behaviours that only becomes big and imposing when viewed as an undifferentiated mass. You then get culture change as the result of behavioural changes, not the other way around. If those behavioural changes come from people who have high social connectivity with others, high trust, or moral non-hierarchical authority, then those changes have more influence on the culture. These individuals can create localised tipping points and others copy the behaviours through imitation in a similar manner to the way fashions are created in society.

Think about who you have in your organisation who could form the nexus of a tipping point, and then work with them and support them. For more information on this approach, visit the website at www.viralchange.com

18. What is the quality focus?

The way an organisation approaches the issue of quality will impact whether learners develop a commitment to excellence, which in turn requires them to use what they have learnt in training courses. People develop a pride in their knowledge and skill set, and their ability to deliver quality, when quality is lauded. People with this mindset in a quality-focused environment will relish the opportunity to learn new skills and apply them.

What is the quality focus of your organisation and how can it help or hinder you when supporting and encouraging learning transfer?

19. Catch them doing something right

Many of the ideas of management grew out of the latter stages of the industrial revolution, where there were careful measurements and a specification of results. Tasks were standardised, and managers saw their job as correcting people who didn't follow the rules and procedures. Our legacy today of this old management style is a legion of managers who think their job is to catch people doing something wrong.

20. What does your onboarding tell people about learning transfer?

New starters in any organisation are at their most impressionable during their first few days and weeks. They are keen to find out about the culture – about the predominant and recurring patterns – so they can use these as guidance to help them operate successfully in their new job. Examine your onboarding process and notice what messages and signals it sends to the new starter about learning transfer.

Ken Blanchard, in his *One Minute Manager* books, uses the simple mantra "Catch them doing something right". It is highly likely that our learner will make mistakes and even, overall, perform less well when they are practising new skills. We should focus on the aspects of what they have achieved that are moving them in the right direction and focus on the effort they are putting in to do something different. Consider how well the prevailing culture will tolerate mistakes made in the pursuit of learning transfer and how you can protect the leaner from the negative consequences of their mistakes.

21. The difference between experience and expertise

An experienced operator is someone who has had substantial exposure to a range of similar situations so that they can discern the inherent patterns and structures. Experienced people then draw on their store of experience to interpret their current situation and find solutions. However, if the situation is new or differs in significant detail, the experienced person may not notice the differences. They may misdiagnose the situation or have, due to the distinctive and specific nature of their experience, a biased view and analysis of the situation.

On the other hand, an expert is someone who has added capacity for reflective evaluation. In other words, the expert has both experience and the ability to judge the level of objectivity of their knowledge. The expert draws on extensive external and structured evidence from research and not just from their own experience. Additionally, the expert is continually updating their knowledge about the topic from external sources and thinking about the connections between their experience and these sources of new information. In effect, the expert is a student of the situation who is questioning and challenging their own interpretation of the situation at hand.

Story: Generic approach in the military
Contributed by: Col Garry Hearn OBE
Note: *Colonel Garry Hearn has over ten years of military education experience following 30 years of operationally related experience. Whilst the views expressed below are not necessarily the endorsed position of the Ministry of Defence or the UK Defence Academy, they are based on extensive experience in delivering training and education in the military domain.*

The military environment has a formal process known as the Defence Systems Approach to Training (DSAT). This process identifies and determines that there is, or might be, a training or education deficiency that needs to be closed with some form of intervention. This is determined by the Training Requirements Authority (TRA), which is normally part of the operational department; thus, ensuring any training and education intervention is based on an operational need.

To a large extent the training design and delivery organisation simply accept the deficit and requirement and provide an appropriate formal intervention to make people competent (not necessarily capable – this only occurs when many other elements align, including informal learning). The responsibility for ensuring the intervention has a tangible impact, or could be considered value for money, is therefore the responsibility of the operational domain and not the person who delivers the training. Albeit, the training deliverer will attempt to deliver an effective intervention in an efficient manner.

However, the reality is that for all the very good reasons articulated by many over the years, regardless of the various theoretical models, it is extremely difficult to determine whether an intervention has had a tangible and acceptable financial value-based impact for the good. Having been involved with a number of non-military learning and development professionals, I would offer that this is not unusual.

It appears to me that, unless it is a very basic level skill such as an organisation needing someone to be able to tighten a bolt without which they cannot sell a product, it is hard to clearly identify the direct correlation between training and value. This is because in most cases the training or education intervention is only one part of creating capability.

In the military this is very much the case with most training being a *series* of activities that, when *combined*, creates competence, not a single training incidence. Additionally, when an individual completes their training they enter a world of complex context that also adds to creating capability through informal experiential learning. Therefore, to clearly correlate training or education incidences with value for money is fraught with difficultly (as it appears is the case in many sectors despite the many theories).

The consequence in the military is that there is less focus on whether it is value for money and a greater emphasis on trust and reliance on the identification of the initial requirement or deficit being correct. In short, there is a sort of acceptance that if we are conducting training or education, there is a requirement for it, because our DSAT processes de-risk the likelihood of this not being the case.

Perhaps more importantly for the military is that we rely on seeking feedback from employers and trainees through a formal external validation process. This is an approach in which the views of both employer and ex-trainee are sought. The aim is to find out how much and to what extent the training is being used (trainee question), and whether the employer has seen an improvement in the individual or organisation. These results are used to adjust training and education interventions due to direct feedback from the operational domain and not from the finance department.

The reality of the military external validation process is that it is not perfect, as is probably the case with most sectors. In our case it is hampered by two factors. First, the employer is unlikely to be aware of a formal measurement approach such as Kirkpatrick, therefore the evaluation process has to use a less specific lexicon. This may result in a more subjective view. Second, the pressure on resources means that the approach is far from total, and therefore not all interventions are evaluated.

Whilst both of these factors introduce a degree of risk, they are still recognised and accepted as being the reality. As such the military takes a pragmatic approach of not trying to expend energy trying to create a 100% evaluation process. It does however accept that the process is probably sufficiently robust to ensure training and education is effective, or to provide sufficient evidence for change. Clearly, where there is a specific incident or accident in the operational environment a formal evaluation is conducted to determine whether there is a link back to an error or omission in training. That way the military continually seeks to identify and learn lessons.

In my own environment, delivering an eight-month education intervention, I have met many ex-students in their work environment. The great thing is they generally start by telling me how much of the course they have used. It is an uplifting experience and provides first hand anecdotal feedback, which helps shape the understanding of whether the course has been effective. In general, service personnel will soon tell you when training and education is not up to standard; like most in the learning and development world, we just need to listen to them.

Specific Example
Having now worked formally in the military training and education environment for some time my view is that training and education interventions must be wrapped in a complete package of 'why, what, how…and probably when'. Only by doing this can effective learning transfer occur.

In a volunteer professional, and training and education-oriented organisation such as the military, we possibly gain some innate motivational benefits that are not as available to some organisations (not to suggest others are not motivated). In particular, we have a clear unifying purpose and a culture that expects professionalism and a desire to improve. This means that on the whole, service personnel expect to be developed; and this helps when delivering interventions.

As part of establishing an understanding within the students of why we are conducting an eight-month training and education intervention, I remind/inform our students on the first day of the course that the reason we conduct the programme is to "*develop leaders and commanders who win wars.*" It is the unifying purpose; the 'why'.

Implicit in the statement is that we do not want our students
to simply learn the knowledge and skills. We want them
to have the self-motivation to apply and stretch their new
knowledge so that they are better than their equivalents on the
battle-field. After all, most military establishments deliver the
same content, therefore the differentiation must come from the
application of the knowledge and skills.

In our case the aim is to stimulate our students into
recognising that simply taking down notes and completing
the course is not good enough; the learning must be applied
and to the best level possible in order to achieve the unifying
purpose. Furthermore, we seek to get them to recognise that
when they leave the Academy, they have a responsibility to
both their soldiers, and to the country, to be successful in what
they have been asked to do.

The application of the knowledge and skills to the best
possible outcome is not a choice; it is their responsibility. In
doing so our aim is to get them to view learning as part of
the DNA of their role as an officer, not just something you do
when you attend a course.

Moreover, by setting this clear statement of 'why' training and
education is delivered, we can then align our 'what, how and
when,' and as such we believe we can deliver content more
effectively. It also means we can focus our instructors and
students on thinking about their course experience as being
in two complementary inter-active layers. Layer one being
the knowledge and skills, and layer two being the students'
self-motivation to use the top end of Blooms Taxonomy to
exploit their new knowledge in a manner that creates the
intellectual edge so as to be better than their adversaries in
terms of attitude and attributes. It also requires the instructors
to focus their efforts on reaching beyond simply transferring
knowledge and skills, and into stimulation of application and
stretching of knowledge and skills.

In short, and reflective of the difficulties in trying to measure learning transfer, we adopt an approach in which the learning transfer becomes an embedded self-motivated attitude and approach within the student. There is risk in the approach but if we get a sufficient mass of our leaders and commanders adopting this approach, we will win wars.

© Col Garry Hearn, 2018
Contact: garry.hearn@learning-transfer-at-work.com

22. Use alumni from previous programmes

There is a story about someone who was in a difficult situation, a deep hole, and couldn't get out. Nobody could, or would, help him. Then an old timer walked by and jumped into the hole with him saying, "I have been here before and I know what to do. Let me show you".

Consider using graduates of previous programmes to mentor new learners through their programme. This can have many positive benefits for both. In one programme I saw, the mentor was not given their full certificate and pay rise until they had helped another person get through the programme successfully.

23. The Gartner Hype Cycle

Gartner's Hype Cycle is a graphical depiction of a common pattern that arises with each new technology or other innovation. The five phases in the Hype Cycle are Technology Trigger, Peak of Inflated Expectations, Trough of Disillusionment, Slope of Enlightenment and Plateau of Productivity. The resultant curve gives you a view of how a technology or application will evolve over time, providing a sound source of insight to manage its deployment within the context of your specific business goals.

These five phases can also occur when introducing learning transfer, or indeed many other changes. It is good to be aware of where your initiative might currently be on the curve. The basics of the model are in the Wikipedia entry.

24. Do you have conscripts on your training programme?

Every trainer I have ever spoken with has stories about trainees on their courses who really did not want to be there. It is very unlikely that such trainees will participate in follow-up activities and transfer the material from the classroom into their workflow. If they won't do what is required to accomplish learning transfer, there is little point in having them in the classroom or on the programme. How can you make sure trainees on an event know why they are there and choose to be there?

25. Beware of the 'ISLAGIATT' principle

The 'ISLAGIATT' principle is a term coined by Martin Eccles, Emeritus Professor of Clinical Effectiveness at Newcastle University. The letters stand for 'It Seemed Like A Good Idea At The Time'. This principle encapsulates an approach in which the intervention strategy is arrived at before a thorough assessment has been made of the appropriate behavioural targets and what it would take to implement and achieve change in these. Instead, personal experience, a favoured theory or cursory analysis is used as the starting point for intervention design, which often leads the programme down a fruitless path.

26. Introduce another player to the trainee/manager relationship

Some behaviour change may require a degree of soul-searching by the trainee and they may want to discuss this outside their immediate line relationship. In this case, introduce another player to keep an eye on the line manager and be available for 'external' help if a trainee struggles with something that they feel they cannot share with their line manager.

Equally, supporting a team member through a development programme, especially one where there are many and varied follow-up activities, may be a new experience for their line manager. The manager needs support too and, like the trainee, needs to be held accountable for their role in learning transfer. Another person outside the trainee/manager pairing can observe the manager and lend a helping hand where required.

I have heard from some commentators that we should bypass the line manager and provide either internal or external coaches for programme trainees to support the learning transfer process. The reasoning behind this seems to be that line managers are not capable of providing sufficient support. I disagree with letting line managers off the hook for what is their responsibility, but I do see the need to sometimes have another player in the game... observer/mentor/coach.

27. Get visibility of what line managers are doing

It is true that managers don't necessarily accept that their role includes being teachers and coaches, so it's important to support them and make it easy for them. This means that you need visibility of whether the managers are stepping up. Which ones are being supportive, and which are not? Which business units are better at learning transfer than others?

Another option is to get trainees on a programme to become buddies and hold each other accountable for the post-event activities and progress.

Story: Building time for learning transfer
Contributed by: Jon Moon, Learning and Development
Delivery Manager

One of the biggest obstacles I have found to effective learning transfer is the time it takes from the learning intervention to the point where the learning has fully become adopted by the learner and is a part of how they behave.

During this inevitable time-lag, and despite the best intentions of the L&D professional, life turns up and the learners get distracted. They sink back into how things were before and easily stop practicing their new skills/knowledge.

It may be that there is a planned follow-up to the original learning or perhaps an action-learning set, but in the gap between the original learning and these follow-ups it is easy for something to crop up. The reason for this is that it is seen by the learner as a higher priority and they drop out from the follow-up. On one programme that one of my colleagues delivered, the attrition rate was as high as 90% over four months. Yet, every one of the learners will still speak highly of the learning event and its impact even though they haven't really changed their behaviour.

One solution to this that I have been using is to adopt the flipped learning model, where we provide all the information on the topic to be learnt to the learners before they attend the event. The evidence on how successful this is as a learning model is well established. It also helps with learning transfer because we extend the time-line of repetition and refreshing backwards before the traditional start point of the learning solution. We can therefore put the follow-up activity into a shorter time-span post event and reduce the time for distractions to occur.

To see how this assists learning transfer, it helps to imagine a timeline with the learning event at the centre. As we move forward through time after the event, the learning level decays without reiteration, embedding and transfer activities. However, if we provide learners with information before the actual event, the event itself becomes part of the embedding and transfer activities.

Of course, the total time for the transfer remains the same, but during the period before the actual learning event the learners will be actively invested in the learning to come rather than thinking that they've done the important formal training bit. They are less likely to see skipping an action-learning set event as acceptable.

For me it's early days on this but the signs are looking promising.

28. Customised learning

When people are learning from activities in their normal work context, the learning is customised for that individual because of the place in which they are learning. In addition, if they are getting support from their manager, that support will be customised to the situation. There is a lot of talk about customised and personalised learning, and yes, you can use fancy algorithms to deliver selected content. But learning from activities within the workflow is automatically customised and is happening without changing the programme materials for any specific individual.

29. Proportion of time spent

Usually, trainees need to spend more time on the programme after the classroom than they spent in it. Without ring-fenced time for experiment and practice within the normal workflow, it is unlikely that much of the material covered in the workshop will survive. If the new learning is simple and immediately implementable, and people can see an immediate benefit, the learning transfer will probably happen. However, if something is that simple, maybe a workshop was not necessary. A workshop would be indicated where there are complex ideas to understand and discuss, so workshop follow-up will inevitably be complex and require significant time.

30. Cultural memory

Discuss with the trainees how tightly they feel bound by the cultural norms. What you are trying to do is get a discussion going on how difficult it will be to transfer the learning and change in the way that you are seeking. How much does the organisational culture rely on utilising methods they have applied in the past, rather than thinking about doing anything new? In effect, does the organisation use memory as a substitute for thinking?

31. Kurt Lewin's model of change

For change to happen, people need to let go of old habits and structures. This can be difficult, because change leads to a disruption of stable situations. To avoid this uncertainty, people prefer to keep the old situation, with its safety and predictability. Kurt Lewin developed a model of change that has three phases: Unfreeze > Change > Refreeze.

Consider what needs to be unfrozen before trainees will be able to transfer their learning and implement new behaviours at work. What is the glue that is holding together the current behaviours? Look a little deeper: is there a permafrost that a surface unfreeze will not change and that will re-assert itself come winter?

32. The problem with understanding

Many training outcomes are couched in terms of 'understanding', but what does that mean? How can you tell when someone understands something? At best, it implies that you will see them do something or answer a question about it. And even this is subjective. Do they understand the topic like I (the subject matter expert) do? Or more than they used to? And from their understanding, do they draw the same conclusion and act the same way I would? If not, is that a problem, because I am right and they are wrong? Understanding, then, is not a useful term when considering learning or the point at which we have learned something.

33. What barriers do trainees anticipate?

Work with the trainees to find out why they think learning transfer can't be done, and then brainstorm ways with them to deal with the barriers they have identified. Ask how can we...? Ask them what three things they would wish for if they had a magic wand.

What resistance do the trainees expect to encounter? What rigidity in the culture do they think they will need to overcome? What do colleagues think? Here are three questions that will help you reveal some of the barriers.

1. What frustrates you on a regular basis? Go on, play along right now and write down a couple of things before going to the next question. Now...

2. What are you indignant about? Again, write down a couple of things. Here's the big one...

3. What are you tolerating now that used to frustrate you or make you indignant?

Run an exercise in the training event where one group argues why the training will make a difference, and the other why it won't. What can be learned from this and what messages does it send to the trainees?

Story: Lots of random, and very useful ideas
Contributed by: Kaye Vincent, writer and information specialist

- Explore ways to use learning on a relevant task or project as soon as possible. I accompanied a new employee to Adobe InDesign training last year. Her work required instant use of her new skills, and she has made friends with Adobe. For me, on the other hand, Adobe feels like a stranger I met briefly having gate-crashed a party! There is no sense of relationship at all!

- Candidates on training should be encouraged to bring back key learning points for the wider team where appropriate. This will help them focus, and in most cases, distil and remember important messaging.

- If learning is about culture change, everyone needs to be involved. Different levels may be needed, but don't just train a few members of staff and expect effective pyramid training. If they aren't experienced trainers, the message will be diluted and buy-in unlikely. Train everyone – it doesn't have to be a 'course'. We forget that good internal comms is a method of training too, especially if interactive elements can be included.

- What constitutes 'training' as opposed to mentoring or coaching? The latter two often work better to help someone implement a new technique or approach. It doesn't have to be the line manager – it can be another internal expert.

- Follow-up training sessions, or evaluation sessions, are very beneficial. If fully programmed in, with clear objectives upfront, then candidates know there is an expectation and a reporting line involved.

- The employee being trained needs to liaise with their line manager about the training, but the line manager also needs to report to upper management to ensure training and people development have buy-in and support from senior stakeholders. This acknowledgement needs to flow throughout the organisation for a learning friendly culture to exist. Without this, learning transfer is up to the motivation of the individual alone, and can be very hit and miss.

- Above all, line managers need to be positive from the very beginning. Training should never be introduced as a 'have to' or 'must be done'. Training must be presented with enthusiasm, as a gift – which it is. And far better to make it a promise, as far in advance as possible. This way, there is an expectation building and hopefully, a sense of enthusiasm. This may help to carry it through. Sounds obvious, but all too often I have seen overworked managers apologise to overworked employees that training is coming up. This immediately creates a negative pattern and room for moaning. Unless essential to process or task, the training has to be unbelievably interesting and beneficial to overcome this and survive the training room.

- Adding to the previous point, line managers need to 'gift' training in a manner that celebrates the employee. It should not be a put down, where the employee feels training is remedial or to 'repair' lack on their part. Far better to offer training because the employee 'has shown enormous potential' and the manager wants to develop this. Make the person feel they have been picked out as an honour and they are more likely to *want* to demonstrate improvement in return.

- If the culture permits 1:1 sessions between employee and line manager, then formally planning discussion about training pre and post the course is useful. It is important for the employee to see that their manager values their learning. If no-one seems to care about the training you do, why should you care and try to implement the content?

- Organisations need to ensure that they have supporting tools or resources to offer when someone returns from training. For example, templates or forms to make a learned process easy to follow. Enable them, rather than expecting the trainee to come back and initiate an entire new system. Have reasonable expectations and assist the learner.

- After Action Review (AAR) is extremely effective. It can be used formally in a reported way or informally in team meetings with simple verbal prompts. We use another simple technique in monthly team meetings where each member has an opportunity to offer one celebration, one challenge and one reflection. This works well to get the team contributing and sharing – and ideal as a technique post training.

- Sounds obvious, but make sure training isn't dry and boring. One very simple way to ensure learning isn't transferred is to make people switch off while it's happening! Test out in-house training with pilots, or meet the external trainer and fully understand their approach. Too little time is spent on analysing the potential training impact on the individual. No amount of systematic approach will circumvent boredom, no matter how worthy the content. *Make it memorable if you want people to remember.*

- A big 'YES' to explaining the 'why' of training. How often is this missed? And just stating a SMART objective isn't enough (often tedious). What difference the training will make is important, but more than that, why is this difference necessary? In other words, what difference does the difference make to the bigger picture (finance, productivity, impact, resourcing, output, time)? And what does the candidate personally expect, prefer, need?

- In performance consultation, ensure there is adequate room to truly acknowledge the tasks people are already good at and do well. Celebrate and confirm this. They may be more receptive to analysis of gaps and areas for improvement if their existing efforts have been positively identified. And if this impacts on their sense of pride, they will be more likely to want continued recognition, which means greater chance for implementation of training in the workplace and learning transfer.

- What if the learning transfer is too good? It can be difficult for line managers to deal with a star student. They send an employee for training to get better at a task, but what if that employee returns and wants to change a process the line manager developed and is personally proud of? There may be a better way to do things, but it can hurt. Sometimes line managers need coaching on how to welcome change from the ground up, just as much as how to deliver change themselves.

- Perception on quality of life is largely about whether expectation matches reality. If the expectation repeatedly falls short of reality, a person's view of their quality of life may not be as high or as stable as desired. The same applies to the workplace. Having a clear set of expectations enables measurement against reality, and to determine quality of performance. But are the expectations in themselves realistic? Performance consultation, or gap analysis, is important to trigger a rethink in this area and set expectations that are feasible and achievable. Training and learning transfer are about resetting the reality.

- Include evaluation of training in yearly appraisals, but change the appraisal process to explore the approach, methods and attitudes, rather than just ticking off a checklist of tasks or projects. This enables far deeper discussion about abilities and performance. Ask the employee to prepare for it themselves, forcing them to do the analysis.

- Learning transfer is the optimum result, but don't make it feel like an imperative. For example, inventing additional projects (often non-essential as a result) to test out or push the learning, can overwhelm an already busy schedule. We should never lose sight that training is there to make our working lives flow more easily and encourage a more effective output. If training and assessment override the work itself to a high degree, with endless reporting and additional paperwork, there may come a point where it meets a brick wall. Again, learning and training should be given and received as a gift. Resentment doesn't empower the individual or the workplace.

Finally, we are constantly learning. Perhaps we need to accept this as the norm, then it's not about transfer, but 'alchemy'.

Training isn't just a course, it's assimilation of knowledge and practising skills. It's what you do every day in the workplace.

© Kaye Vincent, 2018
Contact: kaye.vincent@learning-transfer-at-work.com

34. I want them to stop doing that!

Some behaviour change outcomes are couched in terms of what a manager wants their team to stop doing, but without any indication of what people should do instead. Stopping something leaves a vacuum, and the thing that fits that vacuum perfectly is (you guessed it) the old behaviour. Instead, create a new behaviour. Ideally, design the new behaviour so that doing it means the old one cannot sneak back in.

35. Access to digital platforms

Make sure that trainees, managers and any observers, assessors and interested parties all have access to any digital platforms or systems that will be used as part of the programme scaffolding. Is their access easy? Do they know how to use the platforms that are available as part of the process? What do THEY say is missing from the digital scaffolding?

36. Replace learning objectives with performance objectives

In many training programs the starting point is a set of learning objectives, which are often set out at the very beginning of the training event, just after the icebreaker. Wouldn't it be better to replace these learning objectives with performance objectives? A performance objective describes what the learner will be able to accomplish after a period of learning and practice. It also makes it much easier to align the programme objectives with executing the business strategy, and for these objectives to be seen as aligned by the stakeholders. This focus on proficiency would enable the trainees to filter the information you are giving them for the bits that would help them meet those performance objectives in their job role. Performance objectives should be front and centre during the training programme, and every element of the programme should be linked to them. When you use performance objectives, what message do you send and how does this differ from the message sent when you use learning objectives?

37. Commitment!

Long-term action happens through commitment, especially if motivation waxes and wanes. When someone has committed, and stays committed, they will act even if right now it isn't on their favourite tasks list.

That sense of commitment can be driven either internally or from external pressures. It is internal if the person acts knowing that it is the right thing to do, even if they don't feel like doing it. (Think of that early morning exercise in the rain or declining that extra helping of pudding.) It is external if they act because of the consequences of not acting. This can happen when they are held accountable by their manager, or when they simply don't want to be last amongst their peers.

How can you generate either internal or external commitment in each of the stakeholders who need to act to produce learning transfer?
- Let all the stakeholders know how they will be held accountable, and the consequences of not stepping up.
- Have people make pledges and even sign them. For example, get each trainee to have their manager sign a pledge on how the manager will help and support the trainee through their learning transfer process.
- Make the actions of people visible, so they are aware of their 'audience' and how this will affect their reputation.
- No one wants to be last, so help them avoid this embarrassment.
- Ensure they have clarity on what they are committing to and believe they can do it.
- Ensure they have all the support they need, so they cannot use lack of support as an excuse not to act.

38. How did the manager learn it?

Find out how people have traditionally learned the knowledge and skills your new programme will impart. Maybe they just always learned as they worked and picked it up from experience. Maybe they went to a standard training course that they still consider essential. If the teams and managers still think the old way is the 'best' way to do it and there is no need to try some fancy new-fangled way of teaching, you will need to help them understand how your new way is better for them. How will they benefit from a learning transfer programme?

39. Qualifications?

Does the programme lead to a qualification? If so, is this considered a bonus, or is the qualification mandatory? Is the outcome of the programme purely the qualification, or is there a parallel outcome of behavioural change in the workflow? If the qualification is the key outcome, the programme needs to be focused on getting people through their assessment process. If, however, you want behaviour change, then you should be designing for learning transfer. Or is it both?

40. Hide and seek

How can you find out which trainees are 'not changing'? The way that training is traditionally delivered, with little follow-up and little accountability for change, makes it very easy for trainees to hide from any scrutiny after the event. In fact, they don't really need to hide, because they are pretty much invisible anyway since nobody is looking. When (not if) you start looking and put measures in place to check on their progress, who is to be held accountable? What are the consequences?

41. Check the incentives in place

What incentives are in place that might promote or inhibit learning transfer? These might, for example, be sales incentives, team bonuses, or even competitive team/shift behaviours. I was asked many years ago to do some training for a sales force to help them become more collaborative when working on their major accounts. I asked about the sales incentive scheme and discovered it was biased towards individual rewards rather than team effort, and was mandated by HQ in the US. I turned down the job, knowing I couldn't do what they were asking while that incentive plan was in place.

Story: Lunchtime sessions, bring learning closer to work, collective experience
Contributed by: Joe Tidman
Head of Learning and Development, Johnson Matthey

Lunchtime sessions after training:
At my last company, one of the best examples of leaders being actively involved in Learning Transfer is where a site director I knew intentionally ran sessions every month, over lunch, with first line leaders having recently gone through the programme. He teased out what they had learned from it, practical implications etc. All the while reinforcing the importance of the lessons, and role-modelling the behaviours, and all for just one hour a month.

Bring learning closer to work:
On the ideas front, I have a view to share. It's around the challenge of the in-congruency of the 'classroom', no matter how swish, and the workplace. For even behavioural changes, the classroom space is just not a replication of the office, manufacturing line, lab, etc. That people will go back to when returning to their workplace. Therefore, to aid in learning transfer, I would suggest getting the formal learning activity as close to the real-world as they can. Either actually in it (if technically possible), or beside it (via line-side areas, or using other physical learning spaces), or by replicating as well as possible scenarios in the classroom to replicate the office etc. that they normally work in.

The environment is so critical to those mental muscle memories that drive instinctive behaviours, and it will un-pick the new learned behaviours as soon as they go back into that office. Other options include use of actors to create real-life scenarios in the classroom that the attendees can then interact with and role-play with. Where budget allows, have coaches follow the individual around, and give in-the-moment feedback on key areas whilst they are going about their daily work (might only be viable for execs or high investment high potential employees).

I've seen these all work really well at different times. The key is to match and mirror real-world scenarios. I learned the most about driving by experiencing different roads and driving conditions, not reading my theory manual, or the car manual. The hazard simulator (which used real-world footage) was also a very powerful mechanism, as it replicated my instinctive responses, but in a safe environment.

Collective experience:
The other idea is around the power of collective experience. One of the biggest challenges organisations have with formal learning, is the multitude of suppliers, courses etc. That everyone goes on. The learning impact is very personal (i.e. it's all about each individual learner), however the reality is that conformity bias impacts massively on how people behave. Having experiences that impact on whole populations, including senior leaders (ideally led by them) is far more likely to be sticky, than each of those people going off on their own journeys.

The reason is reinforcement, common language, the ability to talk about the learnings with a group of people who have gone through the same experience. People can pick up things they have missed via other people (everyone remembers different things, and through discussion it reinforces and reminds others of the bits they didn't remember) and the collective experience fundamentally plays to that biological desire for people to feel included, and 'part of the gang' around the learning experience.

It's not always possible, feasible or desirable to do this, but for some applications, having a large group or intact team go through a common experience helps drive behaviour change and retention of knowledge.

© Joe Tidman, 2018
Contact: joe.tidman@learning-transfer-at-work.com

42. What is the appetite for change?

When designing for learning transfer, you must think about the appetite within the organisational culture for change. Do people feel that change is needed? Have people been subjected to so much change that they have what is often termed 'change fatigue'? Do the managers fear change? Or their bosses?

It is often said that people don't like change, but the reality is that people don't like change when it is thrust upon them. How can you involve groups of stakeholders, including the trainees, in the design process, so they feel that, at least to some extent, they have a level of control?

43. Is there a blame culture?

Are mistakes accepted, or just tolerated, or are they a hanging offense? Inevitably, mistakes will occur as people experiment during the learning transfer process. How will the culture view those mistakes? Do the experimenters get a soft or a hard landing? What risk do the trainees perceive in the training follow-up activities? Is there fear in the culture? Distrust? How can you allay those fears or set up a safe zone for experimentation?

According to Carol Dweck's mindset model, many people see failure as a bad thing, while others see it as a route to learning something new. The same applies to organisational culture. How does the culture of your organisation view failure? Does the culture have a fixed or a growth mindset?

44. Scaffold first, then building, then room by room

When designing a house, if you are good at designing kitchens, you may be tempted to start with a kitchen design first. Don't. Start with the house. Think about the outside shape and rough design, then the foundations, and also think about the scaffolding you will need to support the building process. You may need to come back to the outside design as you design the details of the rooms, but the changes should be minimal. Think about how this metaphor applies to building a learning programme.

45. Wean them off spoon-feeding

In many cases, employees will be used to the traditional spoon-feeding techniques of training. How can you design your process to wean them off this spoon-feeding, so they wield their own cutlery and become more self-sufficient in their learning? What do you need to teach them, so they understand more about how they learn in the real world? What awareness of learning do they need to have?

The 70:20:10 model can be useful to help people understand that most learning happens in the workflow. People need to have an awareness of when they are learning, because most of the time they are completely unaware. For learning transfer to happen, the trainees should be aware of the different ways they learn, and particularly that they are learning while they are working, and not just in the classroom.

46. Don't sell learning

When an employee chooses to follow their leader down the road that involves change, they seldom think of the word 'learning'. They think in terms of what they need to do, or what they must find out to get the job done. The word 'learn' can seem like overkill in this context of just finding out what they need to know for as long as they need to know it. 'Learn' also seems like something permanent, whereas people tend to see knowledge as transient. Employees don't typically seek learning for learning's sake. In their mind they want information, skills, tools, tips and techniques they can use to make their life easier and get the job done. We might call that learning, but they usually don't, so don't try and sell them 'learning'. They won't buy what they don't think they want.

Learning may be what they need, but it is not what they think they want, so you should dress up what they need in clothes that make it look like what they want. It is basic marketing. Get your marketing friends to go through some basic marketing steps with you.

- Who is the audience?
- What problem do they have that your offering can address?
- Do they know they have a problem that needs solving?
- What do they think they want?
- Why should they get it from you as opposed to somewhere else?
- What benefits and results do they get?
- What testimonials do you have?
- How do you need to package it, and name it, so they buy?

As well as marketing your initiatives directly to people, you also have a powerful sales force available to you if you can harness it. They are your managers.

47. Involve managers in the design of the training programme

In some ways, engaging the managers of the trainees with the programme is more important for learning transfer than engaging the trainees themselves. Think about it from the manager's perspective. For them, it means change, and one of the fundamental things we have learned repeatedly about organisational change it that it seldom works if you don't involve the people who will be subject to the change. We don't like change thrust upon us, but we will support change if we feel we have had some input into it, and control over it.

How many times have you heard stories of managers who contradict the content of a training course, saying it was too theoretical, or not the way that they were trained, or simply out of date? How many times have trainees returned to their desk and been told, "You haven't got time for all that fancy new stuff, you have work to catch up on"? Managers have an amazingly powerful veto on your programme and they will use it, either implicitly or explicitly, either consciously or unconsciously, if you don't involve them in the early days of programme design.

48.   What does your L&D strategy say?

Your L&D strategy (you do have one, don't you?) will provide some high-level guidance and possibly also constraints on your programme design. I sincerely hope there are statements in the L&D strategy about learning transfer and its importance as part of any learning intervention. If not, right now is a good time to revisit your strategy!

Since you are looking at your L&D strategy document, give it the three-elephant test. Go through it with a highlighter pen and mark any sentences that directly refer to any of the three elephants: Learning Transfer, Performance Diagnostics and Informal Learning. When you are done, how much colour do you have? Even if you have lots of highlighted sentences, do the actions of the L&D function truly reflect the strategy?

Story: Being realistic about learning transfer activities
Contributed by: Tanja Walser
HCM Professional Services Director at Talentia Software

One of the thoughts that struck me while reading this book was that at my last organisation there was an ongoing debate about how the participants didn't have time for learning transfer and, admittedly, I struggled with it myself as a participant. The time pressure when returning from a course was too high to reflect and apply. If that was true for somebody in an HR/L&D role, imagine what it was like for the front office roles.

Looking back after 10+ years in consulting where we know that "your client won't adjust to you, you will need to adjust to your client", I think it wasn't realistic for L&D to tell participants and their managers to make the time. In my view, it's L&D's role to design the performance support in a way that works for the business and not make the business work in a way that suits L&D. I'm saying this 10 years later and after 10 years in consulting where the mantra always is "your client won't adjust to you, you will need to adjust to your client – as much as possible while protecting your project".

© Tanja Walser, 2018
Contact: tanja.walser@learning-transfer-at-work.com

49. What do people really need to 'learn'?

There is a threshold of knowledge and skill that people must reach for them to successfully step up to the desired new behaviours. What is that threshold? Many programmes are designed with the help of subject matter experts who have an inflated sense of the knowledge and skills required to do a job well. What is the real minimum now, and how might that change as people progress with the implementation of their new skills?

Also separate out what people must have memorised and have available on recall, and other knowledge they can quite reasonably look up when they need it. This means that one of the things they must learn is how to use the various support resources that are available.

When deciding how much information to put into the actual training event, how much is too much? The minute someone reaches cognitive overload, they stop learning and potentially lose some of what they have learned up to that point. There are limits to what each person can process, and then transition from short- to long-term memory. There is a strong temptation, given the cost of putting people in a classroom, to give them everything you can within the time available. Resist this temptation. Remember that you are designing an end-to-end process, where the desired result is an improvement in performance, not just that people have seen some new things.

50. Newbies forever?

Some tasks are done so frequently that workers learn to do those tasks from memory. Think of the way you use a piece of software, such as a word processor.

The parts of the application you use often are familiar and you can use them almost without thinking. From time to time you need to use a different part of the application. You don't really use it often enough to remember much about it, so when you do use it, maybe every two or three months, you need to look up the help file or follow a job aid you scribbled for yourself the last time you used it. In effect, you are a perpetual newbie in these less-frequently-visited parts of the application. Requirements for assistance will vary depending on your trainees' familiarity with the task, so any performance support that you build into the programme needs to take this into account. Consider each skill being taught. When the learning is transferred, will it be into a frequent-usage or a perpetual-newbie scenario?

51. Think of it as experience design

Experiences change us. In fact, if you think about it, experiences are the only things that change us. We change as we react to what we experience. Learning transfer is about change, so if you want people to change, you need to design experiences for them so their reaction to those carefully-designed experiences will be the changes you want. Think of what you are doing as experience design rather than learning design, or even worse, instructional design. And since you are designing the experience, make it a good one.

Be careful of the pitfall of assuming that other people are like you and will therefore react to your carefully-designed experiences the same way that you would. They won't. Everybody has a unique set of prior adventures that have made them who they are today, so you need to test your designed experiences on a pilot group. Do their reactions to the experiences fall within the range that will generate the changes you are looking for?

52. Modelling excellence

In almost all training scenarios, you want your trainees to operate at a higher level that has already been achieved by other people. Rather than making assumptions about how those experts operate, do a modelling exercise. Seek out both excellent and adequate performers to model, as this will help you find the difference that makes a difference. As jobs have become more complex and knowledge based, a methodology known as cognitive task analysis (CTA) has emerged. CTA is a technique for uncovering the cognitive processes, such as decision making, problem solving, memory, attention and judgement, involved in performing a job. CTA identifies, from experts, the cognitive strategies and patterns that trainees must learn to perform effectively. Papers and primers on CTA are readily available on the internet.

I often see a training programme that has been stitched together on the basis of a whole raft of assumptions made by L&D, subject matter experts, and others who don't have the skill set themselves. Modelling involves far more than just finding out what people know to do their job. You need to find out
- the minimum information/data they need to have memorised
- the minimum set of practised skills
- what they believe about themselves
- what they believe about the job
- what support they get to do their job
- what barriers they have learned to overcome to do their job, and how they do that
- what aspects of their environment help or hinder them
- any prior experience they deem valuable
- what they consider is common sense, but is not so common
- what they do with conscious competence that others find difficult.

Another big advantage of modelling is that you have exemplars, so trainees know that what they are being asked to do is indeed possible. This is not some theoretical perfection dreamed up in a laboratory; this is real and achievable change. Ensure that the trainees have access to the exemplars, in person if possible, but if not, by video. The trainees will automatically be doing their own unconscious modelling project, because that is how we are built to learn.

53. Practise mixing skills

Training is often done on a skill-by-skill basis, where each skill is taught in turn. The problem is skills are not used this way in the real world. A call centre worker needs to use their rapport and communications skills at the same time as their computer and product manuals, while running a problem-solving routine in their head, and yet these different skill sets are often taught separately. Teaching the skills via scenarios that mimic the real way they are used together 'shortens' the distance of the required transfer.

This is one of the blind spots of competency models that tend to focus on knowledge, skills and attitudes in isolation. Think about the tasks that need to be performed, and how you can define proficiency at those tasks that may well involve a mix of skills being used simultaneously. The raw material for thinking about proficiency comes from your original performance diagnostics process and the behaviour gap that you identified. In effect, if you are to understand how to train people, you need to build a proficiency model for the job for which you are training them. Your design can then move from the proficiency model to learning outcomes to practice activities that will generate the required proficiency.

54. Managers can provide insights that no one else can

Managers have a unique perspective on what it takes to do the job; indeed, in many cases they have done the job themselves before their promotion. This does not mean that each manager is always right about the job, but collectively they can offer a huge amount of wisdom on what is required of their team members, and therefore what training and practice is required.

They also know what they have in the way of time and skills to input into learning transfer activities. Now, they may not wish to provide this support because it will often mean extra work on top of their already-overfull working day. Part of getting managers involved is helping them understand how learning and practice, and their support, are all critical success factors in improving the proficiency of the team, which has an obvious benefit for them. As well as getting insights from managers, you also need to give them insights on basic learning principles and what it will take to get their people up to speed. They need to understand, and be bought into, why the programme is being designed the way it is.

55. Managers will need support

Managers vary greatly in the skill set they have with which to support people through change and coach them in developing new skills. In fact, many managers will shy away from the very notion of coaching, saying that they have never been trained as a coach; in some cases, they will even say outright that they do not wish to be a coach. Some organisations have done such a great job of positioning coaching as a specialist skill that anybody without training assumes they cannot be a coach. One way around this is to position the manager's role as 'a good manager'. That is, all that is being asked of managers is to be a good manager, which involves supporting the people on their team to be the best they can. Of course, the corollary to this is that whoever is managing those managers also needs to be following the same rule.

As you develop your programme with input from the managers, figure out what support they will need at a detailed level so they can, in turn, support the trainees as they transfer learning. You can even use a 'paint by numbers' approach. For each practice activity you are asking the trainees to do after the training, give the manager a crib sheet of actions, questions to ask, what 'good' looks like, words to use for growth mindset encouragement, and so on. Make this material simple to use, detailed enough to be useful and easy to access. It is, after all, performance support and should follow the rules for good performance support. Think 'be there', 'be quick', and 'be useful'. For any performance support, people want the quickest result from the path of least resistance.

Some managers may need more support than others because of their situation. For example, geographically remote branch managers may need more direct support, and indeed, they may even need to deliver some of the training events themselves.

Story: Reflections from experience
Contributed by: Malcolm Hurrell
Former VP HR in global pharmaceuticals company

The business invested significantly in L&D delivering support to learning through many different forms, including offline training programmes. I think the main learning reflections for me and my colleagues were:
- Learning interventions need to be in response to performance gaps, which in turn have been identified and agreed by the learner with their manager as being

important to the team's key contribution to the business.

- These can be both business content focussed, and also individual talent development focussed, i.e. supporting company identified key talent in their long-term capability requirements.
- Any learning need is owned by both the learner and their manager and as such the manager's responsibilities as a sponsor need to be committed to and acted upon, before and after the training to support and challenge the application of learning.
- Design the learning around real work wherever possible and so support post training by investing time to create 'action learning groups' that live on as a way of creating support and challenge in the months after the training. For many of these groups they continued for 12-18 months beyond a given training intervention and provided a rich source of ongoing learning.
- You referred to the classic 'roll out the senior leader to open the training' idea. We did use this technique particularly well with senior leadership development where the programme was 'owned' by the Senior Exec Team who both participated and sponsored the programme.

© Malcolm Hurrell, 2018
Contact: malcolm.hurrell@learning-transfer-at-work.com

56. Map the training course to the job description

All the trainees on the course will have a job description. Does the content of the course map onto the tasks and responsibilities that are in their job description? The course facilitator should make this mapping clear to the trainees. And if the mapping does not exist, or is shaky at best, you need to do something about it, because you are trying to teach people new skills that in theory may not be relevant to them in their job role. Trainees need to be clear about what they are supposed to do with the new material when they are back at work, and if what they are doing is clearly part of their job description, their manager should be helping them.

By the way, what is in the managers' job descriptions about developing people?

57. Remove barriers – reduce effort

A CEB white paper (*Delivering an Effortless Learning Experience*, 2016) concluded that learning outcomes are more successful when programmes are designed to minimise unnecessary effort rather than to focus on engagement and fun. Their research was focused on the digital learner who is reaping the rewards of an increasing spend – 16% increase in the last three years - on making learning fun, proliferating learning channels and providing learning in a more timely fashion.

Although this has led to better 'happy sheets' and higher reported learner satisfaction, it has not led to an increase in learning applied on the job. According to their survey, only 37% of digital learning experienced in the last six months has been applied to the job. I wonder what that figure would be after six months?

The CEB report states that learners value an effortless learning experience more than other learning characteristics. They state that L&D can improve learning application by a factor of 2.7 by making sure accessing, consuming, and seeing the applicability of that learning is as effortless as possible. They use the phrase: "Development is hard; the experience shouldn't be".

They suggest five steps, as listed below.
1. Understand learners' values: design content around what the learners value, not just what the business needs.
2. Prioritise placement of learning: lower barriers to access rather than increasing the number and diversity of learning channels.
3. Boost career applicability of learning: make learning easier to apply to employees' careers rather than just meeting their immediate needs. In tandem with that, show how the new skills are changing and adding value to the organisation.
4. Prepare L&D staff: develop L&D staff capabilities and mindsets to deliver effortless learning experiences rather than engaging learning products.

5. Measure learning application: measure and validate the impact of learning so that you can enable data-driven decisions about talent and learning.

58. Revive learning from its coma

Given the data on how much learning transfers from the training room into the work environment, we could conclude that learning is brought alive in the classroom but rendered comatose by the time it reaches the workflow. One way to think of learning transfer is the reawakening of that comatose learning in the workflow so it is bright-eyed, bushy-tailed and ready to make a difference. By bushy-tailed, I mean that it moves from the limited dimensionality of remembered information to multi-dimensioned knowledge and understanding.

59. Outputs versus outcomes. Different?

We always get outputs, but do we always get the outcome we want? Too often, we focus only on achieving specific outputs, and this can blind us to other ways of achieving our outcomes. One of the reasons we focus on outputs is because they are usually far easier to measure than outcomes. Look at your learning programme goals/targets. Which items are outputs and which items are outcomes? For every one that is an output, what is the desired outcome? Does the output still make sense, given clarity of the outcome?

60. The myth of forgotten learning

It is a common belief that things we have learned, and then later forgotten, are easier to learn again. Perhaps this is based on the idea that the knowledge must still be in our minds somewhere, but apparently there is no experimental evidence for this. We can be fooled into thinking this myth is true because, after some time, our general knowledge within a domain is often greater. Consequently, we have more hooks and related knowledge, which will make the re-acquisition of a specific piece of information within that domain much easier.

Be wary of the argument that giving people in the classroom lots of content is good because that exposure, even when forgotten, will be somehow useful in the future.

61. Understand your trainees

I was talking with an L&D team about how they had designed their programme to suit the needs of their trainees. What soon became clear was that they had not really got close to their audience; what they had done was retrofit an imaginary audience profile against the training programme they had already developed. Now, it's okay to build a model of an imaginary audience, but your next step is to immediately go out into the real world and verify your model.

62. When have you learned something?

If learning = retention + recall, then how far into the future do we need to be able to recall something in order to say that we have learned it now?

Could you now pass an old exam that you passed with ease many years ago? We cannot really talk about successful learning without also talking about the purpose of that learning, and the purpose depends on the context and the timeframe. I could memorise a phone number right now, use it in five minutes' time, and then forget it. Could I validly call that learning?

Rather than focusing on what people may or may not have learned, focus on what they can or cannot do, and how sustainable that skill is over time.

63. Developing a skill

The essence of skills development is the process of becoming more effective and efficient (faster, more precise, more contextually aware and so on) at a task or set of tasks. To become more skilful is to transition from a lower level of skill (imitation) to a higher level (mastery), where the skill is instinctual. The development of skills often follows the 'see-try-do' methodology, ideally in the context within which they will be used for real, and with feedback from others and from environmental cues that denote success or failure. Skills tend to get embedded as habits due to the frequent practice required to hone a skill. This is good, but it carries with it the danger that when the skill becomes irrelevant, due to changing circumstances, the habitual behaviour will continue despite evidence that it is no longer appropriate.

64. Motivation versus volition

Motivation is clearly a significant factor in learning transfer. So is volition and this may be a new concept to you. It is summed up in this quote from Darren Hardy: "Commitment is doing the thing you said you would do, long after the mood you said it in has left you."

- Motivation is a state, an emotion, and is largely unconscious, whereas volition refers to a conscious act of free will that is more like a trait.
- Motivation drives the process of goal selection, whereas volition concerns how we self-regulate in the pursuit of that goal.
- Think of it as the difference between 'I want' and 'I MUST'.
- Motivation is more ephemeral than volition.

Motivation is often triggered by external stimuli or the expectation of a reward, but such motivation is susceptible to change. More-attractive opportunities may emerge, or obstacles may appear that make the reward seem too small. We also use temporal discounting, so that a big reward in the future can seem smaller than a small, immediate reward, and we get seduced by the more immediate benefit, which may be the comfort of lapsing back into old habits.

Volition, however, implies deep personal attachment to an intention, which leads to a determination to achieve it. Learning transfer needs both motivation and volition from all the stakeholders, not just the learner. How can you bake intention protection into your programme?

Consider this story (you have probably heard before, but is well worth revisiting): the Clerk of Works at the construction site of a great new religious building asked the four stonemasons what they considered their job function to be:

> The first said "I'm cutting stone".
> The second said "I'm carving a pillar".
> The third said "I'm building a great and noble monument".
> The fourth said "I'm serving God and humankind".

He invited the fourth to join him on the management team.

I was in a class at the gym and the instructor was urging us to use slightly heavier weights than we would normally use. He said, "There is no change without challenge". This philosophy doesn't extend to all areas of life, but it does apply well beyond the gym and is a factor in learning transfer. The problem is that challenge usually brings with it some form of discomfort, and we naturally shy away from discomfort. It may be the discomfort of the pain of exercising at your limits, or of going a bit hungry on a diet, or of withdrawal from something we have grown used to but want to stop. At work it may be the discomfort of a difficult conversation with a team member, the discomfort of saying you don't know in front of peers or the discomfort of trying and failing. All too often we give up on our goal when discomfort kicks in. When the going gets tough, getting tough to handle it requires volition.

The path to learning transfer is lined with distractions and obstacles that take attention and energy away from purposeful action. Mitigate the effect of those distractions and prepare learners for the obstacles. For example, deliberately create social pressures with public commitments, challenging deadlines or league tables of progress, or have relevant stakeholders monitor the learners' activities to increase the perceived cost of abandoning the goal.

Story: Praise in prison
Contributed by: Anonymous

I worked as a tutor in the British prison system for 10 years. Aggression was surprisingly rare in the classroom, but breaking through apathy was often a more difficult task. I soon discovered that offering praise was the easiest route to releasing endeavour, far more effective than trying to exert unnecessary discipline – funny that, eh?

Many of the men I taught had never received any prior praise for learning in their lives. Once bitten though, the incentive was there. Although I can't claim this student as my own, I saw one adult in his forties work his way from not being able to read at all, to gaining an Open University degree during those years. A phenomenal achievement.

Did the learning transfer? Yes, he left prison and found meaningful employment, assisting others who were struggling as he had. What helped him? The enthusiastic input from all his prison tutors… with a bit of praise.

65. Identify secondary gain from the current behaviour

People do things for a reason, even if the reason is not clear-cut or obvious to an external observer.

If we want people to change their behaviour, we must give them better and more powerful reasons for the new desired behaviour than the ones that are driving the existing behaviour. Ideally, it must be easier to practise the new behaviour than to fall back to the old one.

To achieve this, we need to understand what is driving the current behaviour beyond the obvious. What does an employee stand to lose with the new behaviour? Time? Approval? Kudos? A sense of control? These 'hidden' benefits of the status quo are termed secondary gain and this can be very powerful but lie hidden under the waterline. Note that the secondary gain might be either avoiding something or gaining something.

66. Scary versus dangerous

Things can be dangerous but not scary, like walking on thin ice when you think it is thick, or scary but not dangerous, like walking a high plank when you are on a safety wire.

Change will only occur when someone is prepared to accept a little scary stuff and/or accept some discomfort. Many people use discomfort signals as a sign to back away rather than engage, and so they limit their ability to change, even if their minds say they want to or should. They get confused between what is dangerous, and what is just scary.

Examine the new behaviours you want people to adopt and figure out, perhaps by asking trainees, whether those changes are scary and/or dangerous, and why they perceive them that way.

Also examine the existing behaviours. It is unlikely that they will be scary, but they could be dangerous if continued.

67. Implications of the SCARF model

The SCARF model, which is of course an acronym, was first published by David Rock in 2008.

- Status, which is about relative importance to others: it is our sense of worth; it's where we fit into the hierarchy at work, both socially and organisationally.
- Certainty, which concerns being able to predict the future and having a sense of clarity. A person's brain uses fewer resources in familiar situations than unfamiliar ones and working with a lack of clarity can increase a person's stress levels.
- Autonomy, which provides people a sense of control over events: people need to feel that they have choices available to them, and a lack of choices (and therefore autonomy) will be processed as a threat situation.
- Relatedness, which is a sense of safety with others: people are social animals and naturally form social groups and build relationships, which, if certain and secure, trigger a reward response.
- Fairness, which is a perception of exchanges between people: if something is perceived as unfair, the brain will go into a threat response.

The SCARF model identifies the five domains that activate the primary reward or primary threat circuitry in a person's brain. We tend to behave in ways that try to minimise perceived threats and maximise rewards, so we can look at a stimulus through the lens of these five domains to try and predict how people might respond to that stimulus.

According to David Rock, "Data gathered through measures of brain activity, using FMRI scanners and electroencephalographic (EEG) machines, or gauging hormonal secretions, suggests that the same neural responses that drive us toward food or away from predators are triggered by our perceptions of the way we are treated by other people". In other words, the brain treats many social threats and rewards with the same intensity as physical threats and rewards.

If a person feels that they are being threatened, their primitive emotional brain will quickly work to protect them, and this neurochemical storm reduces their ability for rational thought, to make decisions, to solve problems, and to collaborate. If people feel that they are going to receive a reward, they will bring more cognitive resources, more insights, more ideas for action, fewer perceptual errors, and have a wider field of view. Clearly, if you want people to experiment and practise to accomplish learning transfer, it is going to be much more beneficial to do that within an environment where there is a minimal sense of threat.

68. Process improvement

Think of your learning programme as a process, like an industrial process, and then apply standard process mapping and improvement tools.

A process can be defined as
- A series of actions by which inputs are converted into *outputs*
- A description of something we do to produce *deliverables*.

Process mapping is a tool that uses standardised flow-charting symbols to produce a diagrammatic representation of a business process. It allows the process to be
- Easily explained to people involved or not involved in the process
- Broken down by activity, responsibility, ownership, dependency, concurrency and value
- Assessed for bottlenecks and critical paths
- Measured for time and resource usage.

Consequently, it helps us to identify opportunities to improve the process.

Map your process as it is currently, and then map the desired process that you think you need. What's the difference? There is a skill to process mapping and analysis, so it is worth studying up on it or getting help from someone with experience.

69.   Joining instructions

Create joining instructions that cover the WHOLE programme, not just the event. Make sure that everyone involved has visibility of the whole programme and what is required. Let people know that there is a plan and make sure they understand how the whole programme is bolted together. It's all very well having a vison of what success looks like, but you also need a plan so that trainees and their managers know what they will be doing tomorrow and the next day. Set people up for the full programme and what is expected from each of them, including trainees, managers, facilitators, sponsors and anyone else involved. They should all know what they, and other people, are responsible for contributing to the programme.

Story: How do you change an elephant into a dassie?
Contributed by: Alan Whitaker
Founder and CEO at The Billion Child Foundation

The rock hyrax, known in Africa as a dassie, despite weighing only 4kg, is the closest living relative to an elephant. Most would agree that changing an elephant into a dassie is a ridiculous notion. But just maybe it is possible.

Long, long ago in the mists of time back in 2014 - pre-Trump, pre-Brexit, pre-Bitcoin, UNICEF requested the Billion Child Foundation (BCF), a charity registered in the UK and South Africa, to train school inspectors in Lesotho to empower head teachers/principals of primary schools to reinvent their schools as centres of excellence.

BCF had, since 2011, trained principals of over 350 schools in Africa to reinvent their schools to become centres of excellence with 96% of schools making good or excellent progress towards this goal. However, as the BCF CEO, I was dubious about the proposed process in Lesotho as most education authorities around the world report that cascade training programmes seldom work.

Included in my concerns was the fact that facilitating a culture change process requires special training and intensive coaching of each facilitator. I also knew from the baseline survey that each teacher and principal in Lesotho schools operated largely independently and to a large extent felt abandoned, unappreciated and unsupported. I also suspected that any change was likely to be resisted by principals and academic staff and that implementation of each school's centre of excellence implementation strategy and monthly performance contracts for all management and academic staff were likely to be patchy at best.

Clearly a new approach to training was required.

A three-step approach for implementation 2015/16 was agreed with UNICEF and the Lesotho Ministry of Education and Training. This entailed:
1. BCF would train school inspectors to facilitate the BCF Schools Centre of Excellence Programme (SCoEP).
2. BCF would, over a period of five months, observe/ coach school inspectors while they facilitated SCoEP workshops attended by principals of the schools that reported to them.
3. BCF would accompany school inspectors as they visited each principal between workshops to monitor progress on implementation and to provide coaching and encouragement to speedily and effectively implement each school's centre of excellence strategic plan, and management systems and leadership skills taught.

And this is where the magic started!

Throughout the world, the visit of the school inspector is often feared or resented by principals and academic staff as the school inspector largely plays the role of compliance officer. It is said that at some schools, teachers even dust the leaves of the indoor plants before the school inspector called!

The role of the inspectors in Lesotho changed from being mainly compliance officers to becoming change leaders of teams at each school. This resulted in the inspector, principal and academic staff at each school all working as a synchronised cohesive team towards the common goal for their school to become a centre of excellence.

Roles of each team member were clearly defined: the school inspector as 'Hope and Excellence Leader', the principal as 'Centre of Excellence Implementation Leader', the heads of academic departments to monitor and coach teachers to ensure high-quality curriculum delivery, and each teacher taking responsibility for timeous high quality in-class delivery.

The key words here are goal-directed activities, discipline, culture (the way we do things at our school), accountability, praise, acknowledgment, support, teamwork, breaking silo mentality, focused energy, strategic alignment and pride.

The sense of being abandoned and uncared for was replaced by a determination to give every child the opportunity to become a well-rounded individual who would succeed after they left school.

Schools became, or made significant progress towards becoming, centres of excellence and the end of year results in December 2016 soared.

Conclusions stated in the report to UNICEF by the Lesotho Ministry of Education and Training

1. This programme was a significant success.
2. The role of the inspector has significantly changed from being a compliance officer to that of becoming an Excellence Leader who empowers principals to reinvent their schools to become centres of excellence. While measuring compliance remains important, this has become only one dimension of their job. Compliance has become incorporated and integrated into the leadership provided by each inspector during their interactions with each principal they empower.

3. This programme does not focus on improving academic outcomes. It focuses on changing the culture of each school to become a centre of excellence. The excellent results follow.
4. Principals acquired the skills to make progress on the journey to reinvent their schools as centres of excellence and in so doing inspired the staff to improve the culture of effective teaching and learning.
5. The pass rate at under-performing schools (which had in 2015 enjoyed less than 80% pass rates) on average increased their pass rates by 54%, while the pass rate of control group of schools declined by 7%. This indicates an overall improvement of 61% compared to the control schools.
6. The number of schools gaining 100% pass rate increased from 3 schools to 7 schools.
7. All, except one school, significantly increased its year-end pass marks.

This programme that I was so worried would fail because little change would be implemented at school level, became a major triumph for all concerned, but most of all for the children of Lesotho.

As this programme is rolled out to all schools in the country, tens of thousands of young children who would never have graduated from primary school will now, instead of joining the ranks of the under-educated, unskilled and unemployable youth, enjoy the opportunity to attend secondary schools.

When leaders become involved with their people and provide conditions where people believe in something bigger than themselves, aspire to great things and do the little things right first time, everyone wins.

Moral of the Story
The elephant in the room – lack of implementation following training – can be reduced to the size of a dassie if managers become fully involved as team leaders in driving excellence. We should never send people on courses, or for in-company training, if we as managers are not prepared to become fully

involved leaders. Leading change and coaching are inter-twined, and, if you are a leader, it is a key part of your job.

© Alan Whitaker, 2018
Contact: alan.whitaker@learning-transfer-at-work.com

70. Design, delegate, debrief

The follow-up tasks need to go through a process of design, delegation and debriefing. When designing learning transfer activities, think like a coach who is tasking a coachee between sessions. What is an activity I can ask my coachee to do that will help them learn what they need to know through experience? Design activities that will do the following:

- Ensure they use material from the training course
- Develop from one activity to the next in a sequence
- Mimic, as far as possible, how the activity would play out in 'real' work
- Help them connect the dots between what they can already do and the new behaviours
- Give them results and feedback for fruitful reflection
- Drive them into collaborative sharing, perhaps on a forum
- Get them to describe what they have done, ensuring that it is likely they have done it
- Introduce a little competition/gamification
- Expose them to the 'real' application of new skills on the job or as close to the job as you can
- Show them how to handle situations that may not often occur naturally in the workflow
- Expose them to the 'audience effect' at level four of the learning stack (see explanation of the learning stack earlier in this book).

Then, of course, the task should be delegated with appropriate risk manage-ment in place. Note that tasks may have a very specific output or may be in the form of 'try this and see what you get'. Either way, as with any delegated task, ensure there is clarity of expectations, so people know what to do and when they are done. Learning transfer is usually more about delivering activities then delivering content. Life happens, and people get busy, so you will need a system, probably digital, to remind people of the activities they should be doing to embed the learning into their day-to-day activities.

When someone has done the task, it is essential that they review their activity. This works better if they are reviewing it with someone who is, in effect, debriefing them on the activity. This is where managers come in, because the ideal debriefer is someone who understands the context and has seen the activity take place. Here are some simple debrief questions:
1. What did you want to happen?
2. What actually happened?
3. What did YOU do that caused the gap, or contributed to the success?
4. What will YOU do next time?

Trainees need to be set frequent activities which, week by week and month by month after a training course, build their skills and embed the required new behaviours based on the course content. Habits only form with consistency and practice. If the assigned activities are not done, it is most unlikely that the new behaviours will materialise.

71. Another approach to debriefing

When he heard about this book, Iain Sturrock sent me the following approach, which you may find useful. At its core it consists of four stages of questions to drive learning out of an experience.
1. Outcome/exception: What surprised you? What happened that differed from expectations?
2. Analysis: What was the cause of each exception?
3. Hypotheses: How might each of the identified causes relate to future situations?
4. Actions: What actions will we/you take for each hypothesis, and who is responsible for them?

72. Projects

Consider whether a project would help each trainee to embed and put into operation the new learning. Make sure that these projects have a measurable and tangible value to the business; this then becomes part of your return on investment evidence.

73. Include the 'why'

Tell the trainees 'why' each piece, each task, is done the way it is. Explain the thinking behind the actions so they understand. This will help prevent them from making mistakes that can happen if they are doing things by rote, without the rationale. It will also help them suggest viable improvements that honour the rationale. And if you can't explain to them the reasoning behind why things are done a certain way, perhaps you need to get it clear in your own mind. Don't just teach the actions... teach the thinking behind the actions.

This helps with learning transfer because the desired new behaviours seem more sensible and obvious.

74. Stress and regress

People in stressful situations often revert to what they have done before and cling to past practices as a way of coping. If there is already significant stress in the workplace, trainees are unlikely to be going forward to try new things, even if those new things are designed to alleviate the stress. How can you help trainees deal with the current stress long enough to take on and benefit from the new behaviours, overcoming any additional stress this may at first cause?

75. How to train a dolphin

The hoop starts on the bottom of the pool; when the dolphin swims through, it gets a reward. The hoop is raised ever higher; when the dolphin goes through the hoop, it gets a reward. If the dolphin does not go through the hoop when signalled, it gets no reward. BUT, it does not get punished or chastised. It is given time to think. Eventually, the hoop is high above the water and we see a spectacular performance. So, a complex task (for a dolphin) is broken into stages and positive reinforcement given as each stage is mastered. I know your trainees are not dolphins, although that could be rather fun, but how can you use this principle for learning transfer?

Story: 12 tips for external trainers
Contributed by: Hilary Cooke, Merlin Consultancy

I run extended programmes with participants that attend from the same industry but different employers, so I don't have any real contact with their managers – which is slightly different from the in-company scenario. Learning transfer in between training blocks is vital to create and maintain change and development. Here are some things that work for me, in different strengths and combinations:

1) Reframe the situation - how do you get learners to use their learning to engage and support their line managers? Ask them and challenge them about how they are going to do this in practical ways. What would they like to do and what would get them some benefit? If they are serious about their learning, then negotiating the right level of support is an important skill set muscle to exercise.

2) Then get them practicing what they will do while they are in the learning environment and before they return to the world of getting their own coffee and answering all those emails...

3) I build in a 'how have you shared this to the benefit of your manager and/or team?' question into each post-block review some days after they return to work. If they can articulate it, then it is more likely they have done it, and once they know what is coming next because...

4) When we reconvene, I randomly pick a few learners at the beginning of each block to share, publicly, what they have done with their line manager since the last time. This soon gets some gulping going on!

5) At the beginning of the programme, the learners all prepare a 'this is how I want to be at the end' poster. It gets handed back, folded up and sealed in an individual envelope. Every now and again I make a big show of tantalisingly getting the envelopes out (still

sealed) – or taking a photo of the envelopes, which then subtly appears as a slide pic just before a break; I am constantly nudging them with their own learning journey responsibilities.

6) I set them up with pre and post block templates for manager meetings so that the onus is on them to track down their manager to complete it with them. Even better if you can get them to put dates in the managers' diaries too and set up their calendar for the duration of the programme.

7) At the beginning of the programme, I send each manager a breakdown of the learning and the sorts of benefits they should be able to gain in the business. I also add a list of things that they could get their delegates to do to gain further support and learning. For example, getting them involved in the budgeting process, or taking them along to a sales meeting, or getting them to chair a meeting. I then send marker reminders at the halfway stage, and as we coast into the close. I try to make it easy for them – they are mostly busy people so don't always have the time to think of stuff for themselves, but will happily execute if the benefit is neon lit or the point is ... pointy.

8) I set projects that require project sponsors from the business and have direct and tangible benefit to the business. Apply belt, braces, chewing gum and string to hold it all together so the canyon between theory and practice is as narrow as possible (and can be nimbly hopped across in the dark).

9) Run the odd online forum and invite their managers to share knowledge and answer questions. Keep them short and very pointy. Once it's done, it's done, and the line managers can go ... back to the line.

10) Set up reverse mentoring relationships so that learners are mentoring each other's managers (with obvious boundary management, and with a big fat fancy public award for the best 'mentee manager' if appropriate).

11) Make it fun and easy to engage with us and our learning community. Include line managers at the beginning and

at the end of the programme. Bring cake – they'll come if you make it worth their while.

12) Give each participant a stack of postcards that they can write to their manager at particular way-points on their journey. It can be literally "Wish you were here to share…"

© Hilary Cooke, 2018
Contact: hilary.cooke@learning-transfer-at-work.com

76. Who do the learners copy?

You may think of them as leaders, even when they don't consider themselves as leaders. These are the employees who tend to set the tone and the culture because other employees copy them. Maybe they have been employees a long time, or maybe they have influence because of seniority. They are seen as exemplars of how things are supposed to be done. Do they embody the new behaviours the training course is designed to engender?

77. Task variation in the classroom

The more variation you can introduce into exercises and tasks done within the classroom, the more likely you are to recreate a scenario similar to one the trainees will encounter when they get back to work. The closer the exercises are to 'real-life', the nearer and easier the transfer will be. Practising on a variety of tasks will quicken the learning process within the class and set trainees up for better learning transfer.

78. What do people learn after the classroom?

There is a gap between leaving the classroom with new information and becoming proficient in using that information in a work context. What must happen in that gap, so people move from knowing about something to using it?

One way to find out is to ask people who have crossed that gap successfully. Here are some questions:
1. What did you learn after you left the training?
2. What are you doing now that you couldn't do before?
3. How did you learn to do it?
4. Could you have learned it earlier?

Notice that the last question is designed to help you find a way to reduce the time it takes people to cross the gap. The quicker they make the transition from training to proficiency, the better the return on the training investment.

79. How will you design for the Ebbinghaus effect?

Hermann Ebbinghaus, credited as the first person to systematically study memory, is best known for his discovery of the forgetting curve and the spacing effect back in 1885. The trainees on your programme will steadily forget most of the information they were exposed to on the training course unless you add components into your programme designed to counter the effects of the Ebbinghaus forgetting curve.

Given our propensity to forget things that we don't review soon, and regularly, after we first learn them, it can be hard to retain the learning long enough to transfer to the point of work. No matter what you do, a lot of what is learnt in the classroom won't survive the journey. This means you need to get clear on what learning MUST survive the journey to the point of work, then put in place mechanisms, such as spaced learning, to keep it alive until it gets used. Of course, the corollary to this is that you may decide to reduce the amount of training and instead introduce the content directly into the workflow on an 'as needed' basis, thus avoiding the perils of the forgetting curve.

80. Post-training relapse prevention

Yes, I saw this delightful phrase in one academic paper I read to describe the practice of a follow up session to try and prevent trainees returning to their old patterns of behaviour. Of course, this assumes they adopted the required new behaviours after the initial training.

I think that this should start earlier, in the initial training event. Encourage trainees to think ahead about possible situations where newly-acquired skills could be abandoned in their work environment, and to develop strategies to avoid the relapse.

Story: Almost right, but not quite the success we hoped for
Contributed by: Jennifer Hircock, Learning & Development Manager

At the local authority where I worked some years ago, I developed a framework of training specifically geared towards staff at Tier 4 level (the so-called squeezed middle) who were identified as not receiving the same level of development opportunities as other managers. It is well known that many organisations spend a higher proportion of their L&D budget at this leadership level but that desired changes in behaviours can be elusive.

Plans were therefore developed with care. Senior management agreed that it was time to develop our stars and those with high potential.

The project was very simple; it was important to identify early adopters likely to benefit from it. The management team worked with L&D staff to do so this. Management wanted the scheme to be cost neutral, so positive publicity was very important.

Those who came on board were told that they would have their profiles raised and be able to demonstrate their potential in terms of dealing with a real-life problem/issue within the organisation that they could improve or fix. The roll-out was well planned using project management tools; relevant management meetings were held to scope out how the programme would work; we identified relevant sponsors who would own the project they were asked to work on, and we trained those project sponsors in mentoring and coaching; we were clear with managers about the commitment and what they were required to do to support those on the various projects indicating the importance of what we were trying to achieve. We communicated clearly what was involved with those that were selected, including timescales for development – each project would last three months during which time one day per week would be allocated to it; what support and coaching would be available to them; and what was involved in running an action learning set.

We held a launch event where the sponsors and teams (six people in each group) were introduced. The sponsor presented their projects and the required outputs to everyone and then we announced which teams would be matched with which sponsors. We said that there would be regular updates to the management team on progress. The feedback from the sponsors, teams and managers after the first cohort was fairly positive.

However, the feedback on the second cohort from the sponsors, managers and individuals was not so positive. Why? Because line managers did not support their people by backfilling or reallocating some of their workload. The result was that those on the project teams felt overloaded and unsupported and they began to drop out of the project. What started out as a positive initiative fell at the last hurdle. In addition, those selected for the second tranche were probably less committed than the first tranche. Further, nothing had really changed for the individuals on the first tranche, although they had completed their projects, because there was no real place for them to go. While a couple of them were able to get a promotion, they would have gotten it anyway. For the others, the recognition of being involved in the scheme was not enough of a driver, and the opportunity to participate in the scheme did not enthuse those who were thinking of following in their footsteps.

© Jennifer Hircock, 2018
Contact: jennifer.hircock@learning-transfer-at-work.com

81. The performance support pyramid

Consider what support resources need to be available to the trainees as they progress through their learning transfer journey from novice to expert. Then, consider what ongoing support resources will be needed, after they have become proficient through practice.

For performance support, consider the pyramid model. This means you need to do a lot more than just make the existing current procedures and documentation available at the point of work. You should chunk the information and prioritise it in a way that makes it useful at the point of work. The first point of contact with performance support is the apex of the pyramid. This is the small bit of information that will solve most of the problems. It's surprising how many times the help desk gets asked the same question time and time again. If this initial snippet is not enough, they will need to access the next, broader layer of the pyramid, which has more information. Perhaps this time it is a list of frequently-asked questions. After that comes another layer, which could be a user guide or user manual. Under that perhaps another layer again with broader information, and references to other documents. After they have been down these ever-expanding levels of the pyramid, if they are still stuck, the next step is to contact someone who can help them.

Performance support is often consumed in a state of stress when someone is saying "HELP! I'm stuck". It therefore needs to be simple and direct. Give it the 'would a seven-year-old understand it?' test. It needs to be easy to consume, which means you should think about presentation and even things like the font size and paragraph length. (Consider the Gunning Fog Index for readability?) Make sure you create the performance support in collaboration with the eventual end users, who are probably at different levels of experience and expertise.

The pyramid is an idealised situation to be sure, but the concept of providing only enough to meet someone's immediate need, and then more only if they ask for it, is useful. Giving someone access to the full user manual, when all they have is a simple question, is not actually being very helpful.

For more on providing performance support and the support pyramid, see *Performance Support: Strategies and Practices for Learning in the Workflow* (McGraw-Hill, Dec 2010), by Con Gottfredson and Bob Mosher.

82.   Performance support: why as well as how

Have you ever read a software help file that tells you that the button with SAVE written on it does indeed save the current file? User guides, particularly in the software arena, tend to suffer from this problem: they provide a viable description of what the features are, but little information as to why you might use each feature, or the consequences of taking certain actions. They don't give you enough information to decide between actions A, B or C.

Make sure your support resources help people make contextual decisions and support action, not just knowledge. The only way to do this is put yourself in their shoes and ask, "Why would I do X or Y?" or coach someone who has recently been through that learning curve to help write the support. Get it approved by a subject matter expert, but be wary of their approach because they are not a user; they don't need the support themselves and what seems to be common sense to them is not necessarily so to anyone without their experience. They have usually forgotten what it is like to be a novice without their fluency of recall in the subject.

83.   The workplace evolves

Note that the point of work can often be a shifting target. Individual trainees are likely to have subtly different points of work, and those differences will change over time as the workplace evolves. How can you put in place mechanisms of support that will keep up with that evolutionary journey of the workplace?

84.   The five moments of learning need

It is often not just a straightforward case of trainees applying what they've learnt; there are also situations that occur when what they have learnt does not quite fit because the environment has changed, or something has broken and so the standardised response will not work.

Con Gottfredson and Bob Mosher have developed a model that encompasses what they call the 'Five moments of learning need'. They say "An organization is competent to the degree that it is gaining and sustaining effective performance at every changing moment. These 'Five Moments of Need' provide the overarching framework for performers to become and remain competent in their individual and collective work". Their model helps people change from a training mindset to a performance mindset.

1. NEW: when performers are learning how to do something for the first time.
2. MORE: when performers are expanding the breadth and depth of what they have learned.
3. APPLY: when performers need to act upon what they have learned, which includes planning what they will do, remembering what they have forgotten, or adapting their performance to a unique situation.
4. SOLVE: when problems arise, or things break or don't work the way they were intended.
5. CHANGE: when performers need to learn a new way of doing something, which requires them to change skills that are deeply ingrained in their performance practices.

See the model at www.5momentsofneed.com

85. Time is of the essence

Design your programmes so people are required to put into practice as quickly as possible the key knowledge and skills that will make a difference to their performance. The longer the delay, the tougher it will be for them to implement their new knowledge and skills.

Obviously they can't immediately implement everything the next day they are back at their desk, so you need to develop a sequence that makes sense to the trainee and builds one block on top of another.

What about timing? How should the process of learning transfer interact with other projects so learners have the opportunity to transfer? If you train on a new IT system too early before launch, they cannot transfer their learning before it fades.

Story: Some lessons from software training
Contributed by: Agnieszka Scott
Training Manager (software training specialist)

All of us are expected to use software of one form or another.
My experience is that most software learning is done either by
self-learning and/or by learning from peers. It looks like the
70:20:10 model is fully utilised. Not only that, there has been
successful learning transfer – people start using the technology
in their day-to-day work. Goal achieved! So it seems...

There are many users who use their company's IT system
wrong. Very often users work off scripts created by their
colleagues who themselves learnt from their predecessors.
They simply follow instructions: "Click here, enter this value
there, save, open screen ABC". They follow it blindly as they
never had an explanation on why they need to take those
steps and enter specific values. They complete processes, not
because they understand why they do it, but because it either
seems to work after they figure it out by themselves, or they
were told what process to follow.

A lot of software users I've met in a formal training
environment were happy to admit that they don't really know
what they do. Sometimes their errors and incorrect entries are
corrected later in the workflow process by another department
without them even being aware of their mistakes.

Some might say that it is the job of the software to validate
entries, and to a certain extant this is true, but it should also
allow users to make their own decisions – the fine balance
between restriction and flexibility. I used to work with
accounting software and we had this anecdote about a user
who had been shown by a colleague how to use a certain
function: enter a description of what you're buying - in
this case photographical equipment and enter the GL code

– 'Photography'. There was no way the system could validate whether the selected GL code was relevant to the free text description of goods. The user, after the initial induction, kept ordering all sorts of goods/services: concrete, tarmac, lunches etc. and booking them all to photography.

This brings us to the point of the user not being aware of the full process and bigger picture. Scripts, colleagues or other internal resources don't always cover that. Once this user attended formal training where the bigger picture and the whole process was explained to him, he no longer booked all his purchases to photography.

It seems to me that in the software world the formal training is more than 10% in the 70:20:10 model. Or rather, the 10% is crucial to the correct learning being transferred. Informal learning is very powerful but how can an individual extract the best practice from all other, not necessarily correct, messages? In a perfect world of only correct and verified resources, and colleagues who are excellent at knowledge sharing, formal training for software would be redundant. However, in this imperfect world we live in, it is vital not to forget about or underestimate the 10%. Very often it is the only time a user can verify that what they know is what they are supposed to know.

If I had an unlimited budget I would offer a blended training solution for any software training. Users attending training often ask for scripts, videos, additional sessions, documentation. The challenge is that they ask for different things as they all have their preferred learning/reference method. My dream is to have a fully developed learning platform allowing users to access e-learning modules, videos and articles, but for now I need to make do with what I have. Currently, I offer the training in face-to-face and one-hour modular virtual classroom formats. It is encouraging that users are very happy to attend refresher training on a specific subject. They are also happy to follow recordings of sessions and just contact me individually with any questions that may arise.

PS. An example from just yesterday: A user figured out a certain bit of functionality for herself, based on various resources, and started using it. She attended a training session when we spent a moment talking about this functionality. She was very annoyed when she realised that she had it wrong! She said that this issue probably wouldn't be detected for 20 years (and then it will be way too late to rectify it) if she hadn't come to this refresher training session.

© Agnieszka Scott, 2018
Contact: agnieszka.scott@learning-transfer-at-work.com

86. The doctor analogy

If you are the trainer and feel that you have limited influence as to what goes on after the training event, think about the problem a doctor faces. They have a short time in the consulting room and then they send the patient on their way with some advice and perhaps a prescription. It is then down to the patient to follow the advice and take the tablets, read the supporting material, do the exercises, eat the right foods and so on. Having said that, there are some things the doctor can do that will 'stick' better; for example, if the doctor put some stitches in a wound, it is unlikely the patient will rip them out.

Whether the patient follows the advice or not will largely depend on their state of mind and trust in the doctor, and whether what is being asked is easy enough to do. A good doctor will set the patient up with the tools and support that will enable healing after leaving the surgery. A good doctor also knows that healing happens after the consultation, not during it. He has that brief period to do the best he can to set things up so that healing is optimal. He seeks to extend his reach beyond the consultation to influence the patient during the whole healing process.

How can you use this doctor's mindset when you are designing your learning programme?

87. Design to fit into peoples' working lives

So much of the success of learning transfer is based on what people do after the formal training, when they return to their work context. This means that you, as a designer, must understand their work context at a detailed level. You must understand their working lives.

- What could be a reasonable unit of undisturbed time?
- How are they rostered on shifts or time zones?
- Can they get quiet time?
- Do they have IT access?
- Can they schedule stuff ahead of time?
- Are their jobs mostly reactive?
- Blue collar/white collar?
- What would colleagues think of them practising learning activities during the day?
- Do they tend to put in extra time, and is it paid or unpaid?
- Given the prevailing culture, what support will they get from their manager and colleagues?
- If they are delegated tasks, what are the consequences of not doing those tasks?

88. Spacing and repetition

Spaced practice, procedural learning, distributed practice, priming and other methods have a long history of demonstrating greater persistence of learning, resulting in improved performance, and all of these tend to work better when we learn and develop a new capability within the context where we are going to use it. This suggests that a key part of any learning transfer programme should be spaced practice within the workflow.

89. If you are buying in generic training

Generic off-the-shelf training will produce results, but all other things being equal, the transfer rate will be lower than from a training course designed with specific locally-identified issues in mind. This also applies to a custom course that is then rolled out widely to a large population in different regions. It is a sheep-dip approach that will likely take little notice of local cultures and needs.

The sheep-dip approach mostly ignores the learning transfer requirement for high relevance, so trainee motivation will be lower, and this negatively impacts transfer.

Sure, it is easier and probably cheaper to buy off-the-shelf training courses, but do an analysis of what you get from them in terms of business results. Then consider what you could get with a more targeted programme that is fully up to date and pulls all the learning transfer levers.

90. Handouts and training manuals

I know people who use the 'thud' test for course manuals. Does the manual make a satisfying thud when dropped onto a table in front of the trainee? If it does, there must be lots of stuff in there, which is good – right?

When designing the course handouts and materials, think about what the trainees need after the training. After all, the period after the training is more important than the period in the training, isn't it? During their transfer period, what material, and in what structure and format, would help them best? How can you ensure that the support resources will provide them with the easiest and quickest access to just the pieces of content that they will probably need the most, rather than flooding them with other stuff that is not at that time relevant? Then, how can you set up the structure so that they can dig deeper for more information if they need it? Think of a pyramid, where you start at the top and dig down to wider and deeper levels.

Design the manual as a useful transfer and performance support tool and make sure it references any other performance support systems the trainees have available. When you have done this, think about what else might be needed in the classroom. Note, these classroom resources could be separate to the main course notes, so they don't clutter up the course manual after a one-time use.

91. Set boundaries and expectations

After a training course, the trainees need to know that they should experiment and practise, and they should also know where the boundaries are in terms of managing the risk of trying out new things.
- What expectations will you set?
- What boundaries will you set?

How will you keep things safe within those boundaries, for them and the organisation?

Story: End of programme action planning
Contributed by: Jonathan Handcock
Learning & Development Facilitator at Bowles

Our situation is slightly different in that we provide learning experiences often using the outdoors as a vehicle for behavioural and soft skills learning. It is also a different situation as we have a short, privileged time with delegates before they return to their place of work; the implication being that we have limited opportunity for ongoing contact with delegates. As such we have adapted our approach to have the best chance of success for the client in terms of a return on expectations.

In order to lay the best foundations, we find that the most important stage of any intervention is the early meetings with client stakeholders. The stakeholder is often a Learning & Development Manager or a Head of Department. This is our opportunity to really understand the outcomes required and often to challenge the client to ensure their perception matches their overall corporate strategy and organisational values. As long as our client fully buys into their own programme outcomes, then together we have the very best chance of success. This relationship also enables us to have ongoing dialogue with the key stakeholder even though we are unlikely to have this level of ongoing contact with delegates.

One approach we use is to facilitate an action planning session at the end of a programme. This session will combine the following aspects:
- Collated ongoing feedback everyone will have received from any visiting managers, from their peers, and from

us as facilitators. This will have been collected by each delegate during the programme.

- A carefully managed one-to-one peer feedback session. Each delegate will have the opportunity to share "one thing I value about you" and "one thing I think you'd benefit by doing differently". This session is sensitively framed and stage-managed to ensure that certain feedback 'guidelines' are adhered to. Plenty of value comes from this session.
- Small group discussions and or coaching sessions to ensure individuals dig deep and are producing goals/ plans that they truly buy into.

While the wheel has certainly not been reinvented in any of the above, we find that delegates really action their plans when they are produced in duplicate: one for the individual and one for their line manager. The delegates leave us with a belief in what they want to achieve moving forwards and they are now answerable to their line managers (and sometimes to their peers) to ensure this really happens.

Should the situation allow, we run a follow-up session (usually a half-day at their place of work). This is an opportunity for participants to either celebrate what they have achieved to date or to revisit actions that may not be progressing. If the former, our role is to recognise these successes while challenging participants to explore further steps, usually highly motivating ones in career terms. If the latter, our role is to coach them through the situation in a constructive way.

Feedback suggests this process works well and we refine the process to ensure it matches an individual client's values and culture.

© Jonathan Handcock, 2018
Contact: jonathan.handcock@learning-transfer-at-work.com

92. Opportunity or remedial?

The way trainees perceive a programme before they even embark on it has a significant effect on their subsequent learning transfer. Do they perceive the training programme as an opportunity, and therefore desirable, or as remedial, and therefore akin to wearing a dunce's hat in the corner?

One misdirected comment from a team leader could wipe out the benefits, so marketing the programme either directly or indirectly, via managers and supervisors, is a critical part of the setup. Of course, this is much easier when those managers and supervisors are involved from the early stages of programme design.

93. Crossing the Rubicon

Julius Caesar's popularity was a threat to the Roman Senate, which ordered him to disband his army, at that time camped north of a small stream called the Rubicon. An ancient law forbade any general from crossing the Rubicon and entering Italy proper with an army. Despite knowing it was treason, Caesar deliberately crossed over on 11 January 49 B.C. Once he had done so, there was no turning back; civil war was inevitable. From that point, Caesar had a single objective: to win the war. How can you get learners to cross their Rubicon?

94. Practice really does make perfect

In an article in *Nature Neuroscience*, 'Learning by neural reassociation' (March 2018) the authors discuss the temporary shortcuts the brain makes in learning a new skill, and then how subsequent practice generates new neural pathways that produce the ideal activity patterns. They studied intracortical population activity in the primary motor cortex of rhesus macaque monkeys during short-term learning in a brain-computer interface task.

What they saw was, as they put it, completely unexpected. When faced with a new task, the brain is constrained to use the neural activity patterns it's capable of generating right now and use them as effectively as possible in this new situation. It does not generate new patterns, but rather repurposes existing ones. The result is a sub-optimal ability to do the new task. Within the first few hours, it is applying a 'quick and dirty' fix to the new problem it is facing, indicating that the brain may well not be as flexible over the timescale of a few hours as we have imagined.

It seems that proficiency from optimal neural activity takes time and practice, so we need to give people time and practice to perfect their new skills.

95. Change outside the comfort zone

If the new behaviours you want to see people adopt are outside their comfort zone, you will need to sneak up on them. Rather than ask people to step out into unknown territory, where there are dragons and scary things, reach out and pull the difficult thing into their comfort zone. This is a subtle, yet powerful distinction. Think of something that you would like them to do, though it is outside their comfort zone. How can you change it a little so at least a bit of it will come inside their comfort zone? Ask them to do the bit they have 'access' to, and as they do it, more will come into reach. Repeat.

96. Context-dependent memory

In psychology, context-dependent memory is the improved recall of specific pieces of information when the context present at encoding and retrieval are the same. In effect, this means that if I teach you something while you are driving a car, and particularly something that relates to driving a car, you are more likely to be able to recall that later when you are driving a car than if you were sitting in your office. Experiments have been done to show the effect by using simple environmental context changes, such as quiet or noisy surroundings while learning, and then sitting an exam on the material. The idea of context can be widened to also include factors such emotional state, physical states, such as tiredness or hunger, and the presence of drugs or alcohol.

What does this suggest to you in terms of how you can design your training and the follow up activities?

97. Lesson from a chef

Chefs cook food that their customers like. They strive for the joy of those they serve. They take pride in their work and I am sure would like to eat what they have prepared. Would you like to consume the learning programme you are creating? Ask yourself this question, and then ask what would make it even more 'appealing'.

98. Experiments and activities

Learning transfer requires experiment and deliberate practice after the training course, so before it, when you are designing the learning programme, you will need to design those activities. Here are some broad types of activity which you can use to take a concept or idea from your course and create a follow up activity to help embed the concept and turn it into behaviour.

1. Exploration of an idea
   a. What is similar?
   b. What if it was bigger? By a factor of 2? By a factor of 100?
   c. What if we added one more?
   d. What if an extrovert had this problem?
   e. What if the whole situation was reversed?

2. Discovery
   a. Do something and notice the results.
   b. Find something else that has similar results.
   c. Change the parameters and try again.
   d. Do a sensitivity analysis on your data.

3. Justify
   a. Prove your hypothesis with tests and experiments.
   b. How consistent are the results?
   c. What evidence would be needed for proof?

4. Argue
   a. Make a case for your hypothesis.
   b. Teach others what you have learned.
   c. Play devil's advocate.

5. Introspect
   a. What does this mean to you?
   b. How can you use this?

    c. How could you help others use this?

    d. How does it make you feel?

    e. What do you think it leads to as a next step?

    f. What will you stop, start or continue?

    g. What is a first baby step?

Story: Training triangles
Contributed by: Don Morley
Former Training and Development Manager at Natwest

When I took over the role of Training and Development
Manager for the Corporate and Institutional Banking division
of NatWest Bank in 1989, there were two views about the
training function. Some managers felt they were obliged
to send their staff on training interventions while others
considered the department simply added unnecessary cost
to the business. Either way, the overall feeling was that the
process added little or no value. As a result, managers, be
they senior or junior, were largely disengaged with the task
of addressing solutions to underperformance; at least, not by
training.

Very quickly we realised that there needed to be a three-way
dialogue before any training expenditure was signed off. We
dubbed the process 'training triangles' to flag to the business
that no training intervention would be paid for out of the
department's budget unless there had first been a meeting
between the manager, the staff member and a trainer. We
launched the process by making a series of presentations to
all managers to show that the game had changed. No longer
would we be trying to press training on them or their staff; they
had to come to us if they wanted some of our precious budget.

Some resented this, but most found it refreshing that here
was an HR function determined to contribute to the division's

performance, rather than being yet another overhead to be deducted from their hard-won profit. We backed it up by insisting that there be a follow-up meeting after the individual had been on the training intervention of our choosing, to judge how successfully the solution had closed the performance shortfall. A further illustration of our desire to minimise, not maximise, the training budget was that we would refuse to sanction training if the discussion disclosed other issues for which training would not be an appropriate fix. Training for training's sake was no longer an option. Another major break from tradition was evidenced by an outcome that might see the manager's behaviour, or lack of leadership skills, as the determining factor in the underperformance. This would lead to an intervention, not to aid the staff member, but to assist the manager.

Another benefit of 'training triangles' was the way it benefitted the annual performance appraisal process. It stimulated a more frank and focussed discussion now that the training intermediary had widened the exploration of reasons for underperformance during the year. Needless to say, members of the T&D department had to be trained in facilitation skills to get to the root of the problem rather than, as in the past, being seen primarily as a purveyor of workshops or other training media.

At the time the bank was still the largest in the world and practised a very top down management style. This new approach, particularly coming from an HR function, was therefore seen as controversial, to say the least. Managers were not used to being questioned and staff members were often reluctant to 'open up' for fear of the consequences. However, the more enlightened managers could see both the logic and the value of the new approach as the bank began to feel the pressure of competition. The training function was no longer about inputs; the emphasis was now firmly pointed in the direction of outputs.

Perhaps the most telling outcome was that, whereas in the past 'failed' bankers were shunted into HR roles, the training department was now seen by many aspiring young staff as a good stepping stone to a management role. It not only afforded them observational experience in how to manage staff to deliver performance but also had the added benefit of allowing them to impress the management echelon by their skill in conducting effective analysis and implementation of business enhancing training solutions.

The learning from this turnaround project to secure a new reputation for the training and development function can be summed up in a few key principles.

- The first is that it is essential to establish where the problem truly lies in an individual's underperformance and whether training is the correct solution or even part of the solution.
- Next, the nature of the intervention must be suited to that person's preferred learning style and therefore the manager and subordinate must commit to an outcome that is measurable in some meaningful fashion.
- Thirdly, there should always be a follow-up process to judge the value and appropriateness of the training and to ensure that the member of staff, of whatever level, has had the opportunity to put learning into practise.
- Last but not least, there must be a direct link between training and appraisal. If the latter is intended to review an individual's performance over a period of time it surely follows that due consideration must be given to how effectively he or she has been equipped to do the job to the best of their ability.

© Don Morley, 2018
Contact: don.morley@learning-transfer-at-work.com

99. Feedback is essential

We all need feedback, especially trainees on their learning transfer journey, so this needs to be planned into the programme. Imagine trying to explore new concepts or practise new skills without any useful feedback.

- Who will give the trainee feedback at all the steps of the learning transfer journey?
- Does the person giving feedback need support to help them give quality feedback that is timely and explicit?
- Do they understand the importance of their feedback to the aspirations of the trainee and the programme?
- How can you ensure that trainees get feedback from multiple sources and perspectives?

In addition to getting feedback from people, trainees will also get feedback from their environment, as they see the results of their actions and discover whether what they are doing is successful or not. This is fine if the feedback from the environment is immediate and visible; however, in many cases the environment is not so obliging. Take the case of hand washing in a healthcare setting. Hands might look clean even if they are still contaminated with bacteria, so there is no immediate feedback that the hand washing has been successful, or indeed is needed. In addition, there is no feedback from the environment about infection caused by a lack of hand sanitisation because of the delay in consequences. Consider how you can fine-tune feedback from the environment surrounding the learner so that it is both visible and immediate.

100. Adult versus child learning (or pedagogy versus andragogy)

We were 'taught' how to be taught and how to teach at school and our further education years simply by being students in the system. Many say that the education system is nowhere near as good as it could be; in addition to that, adults learn differently to children, so we should let go of 'teaching' as we remember it and focus on how best to help adults learn, and then use their learning.

Adults want to know why they should learn something and tend to be more motivated to learn skills they can apply in their day-to-day life. They are goal-oriented learners, especially in a work context, so they will respond better to problem-centred rather than content-centred development. This also means they need to know WHY they should learn something before they will commit effort to doing so. They are more self-directed and responsible for their own decisions, so it is better to lead them rather than manage them as learners.

Another factor is that adults, unlike children, carry a rich history of experiences, which comes with the baggage of implicit biases and assumptions that narrow their views and beliefs. These can either help or hinder their current learning, and sometimes adults need to unlearn something before they can relearn a better alternative. Consider the effort it takes for someone to start driving on the other side of the road in a foreign country. Many of their automatic reflexes are now an enemy rather than a friend. Einstein said it so well: "I must be willing to give up what I am in order to become what I will be".

101. Agile development of your learning programme

A full-scale learning programme that includes all the components required for effective learning transfer is complex; far more complex than a simple training event. This complexity is perhaps one of the reasons that so few people venture into designing for learning transfer, so let's look outside the L&D space at another industry, one where complex and fast-moving projects are the norm: software. Many of the values, principles and practices of agile software program development can be applied almost without change to learning programme development.

Your first port of call should be the Agile Alliance website at www.agilealliance. org, where you will find their manifesto and their 12 principles, which can be adapted for learning programmes.

According to Wikipedia, "Agile software development describes an approach to software development under which requirements and solutions evolve through the collaborative effort of self-organizing and cross-functional teams and their customer(s)/end user(s). It advocates adaptive planning, evolutionary development, early delivery, and continual improvement, and it encourages rapid and flexible response to change."

Moving to effective learning transfer programmes involves change and a transition period. This entails moving from what is probably a traditional cur-riculum-based training-only event approach to a training/transfer programme approach. Whether you are designing a new programme from scratch, or converting an existing training event, use an agile methodology rather than trying to build a complete design and then launch.

In 2012, Mark Zuckerberg wrote a letter to prospective shareholders in the upcoming Facebook IPO. In it he said, "We have the words 'Done is better than perfect' painted on our walls to remind ourselves to always keep shipping". Many people often fail to 'get it shipped' due to fears of criticism for not getting it perfect.

102. Nelson Mandela on language

"If you talk to a man in a language he understands, that goes to his head. If you talk to him in his language that goes to his heart." - Nelson Mandela

And by language, he does not necessarily mean French or Zulu or Arabic. He means talk in words and concepts that matter to the listener. What is important to them? When you need to talk to trainees about the change in the shift patterns in a factory, don't talk about the financial reasons for the change; instead talk about how the change will impact them. Talk about things like the time they can clock off and how that relates to picking up their children from school. What we focus on gets magnified. So, magnify what matters to your audience. Talk about what they care about, which might not be what you care about. If they know that you know what they care about, they know that you care. Read that last sentence again carefully.

103. What will the line manager learn?

Get clarity for the manager that they will learn too. The best way to learn something is to teach it. Real knowing comes from doing and teaching 'how' to others.

104. Trainees can support their manager

Understand and promote how trainees using their newfound skills and knowledge will support their managers. What activities could you give to trainees to accomplish this?

Story: Effective line managers
Contributed by: Rachel Burnham at Burnham L&D Ltd

When I was in my very first role in-house as a 'Staff Development and Training Manager' (yes, it was that long ago!) I noticed that the extent to which learning got embedded into day-to-day work practices varied hugely, not only from individual to individual, but also from team to team.

I noticed that the managers of the teams I worked with had very different styles of management and some of them made lots of use of coaching of team members. Those managers who routinely used coaching and regular provision of feedback to their team members, were in the teams where learning from face-to-face courses was most likely to be applied in the workplace. And that application of learning appeared to be much deeper and more sustained.

One manager's approach in particular stood out for me. She was a great role model for learning herself, not just engaging with learning from face-to-face programmes, but participating in a major secondment. She freely shared her learning and how she was using it. She engaged in regular and frequent conversations with her team members about what they were learning at work and how they were using their learning. She provided feedback and recognised publicly the learning that team members were doing. She not only coached team members herself, but also encouraged others in the team to coach and share learning. She used team meetings to share and reinforce learning. She didn't just rely on courses to support learning in the team, but encouraged reading, team activities, delegation and tailored challenge projects. She had exceptionally high standards and worked in partnership with me to support the effective performance of her team in every aspect of their work.

I learned a lot from her about how to support the transfer of learning.

105. Set goals at the end of a workshop?

It is common at the end of many workshops to ask trainees to set some personal goals on how they will implement their newfound ideas from the workshop. However, think of the circumstances.

The trainees are at the end of what probably feels like a long day and they are looking forward to going home. Their brains are tired, and they are tired. They are asked to go back over the events of the day, perhaps from the notes or the workshop manual, and construct goals which they then faithfully promise to go and do next week, when they are back at their desk.

This is too little, too late, and often done without them having a good understanding of the overall programme outcomes. Perhaps, with the best of intentions, the trainees will write a few things down to get through the exercise and out of the building. These goals should have been set with their manager, and with full knowledge of the overall programme outcomes, prior to the workshop.

At the beginning of the workshop, discuss the goals they have brought with them and how they fit within the programme, and from time to time during the workshop refer to them in the light of new material covered. At the end of the workshop, you could have them review their goals and perhaps buddy up with someone else from the course to hold them accountable for those goals in addition to their manager.

106. Permission to change

Make sure that trainees know they have permission to change. This needs to be explicit rather than just implicit. How can the executive sponsor help? It is surprising how, in many organisations, people will wait to be told rather than take the initiative, because of the prevailing culture.

107. Who is doing their job?

When the trainees are away from their workplace and in the classroom, who is doing their job? When the trainees are doing activities and tasks after the workshop to practise their new skills and accomplish learning transfer, who is doing their job? What experience do you want the trainees to have in relation to their workload before, during and after the training event? Who has the biggest influence on that experience? Their manager?

108. Nudging the manager

Plan how you will keep managers nudged and reminded of their commitments regarding learning transfer for what might be quite an extended period of many months after a training programme. It is all too easy for managers to get lost in the hurly-burly of day-to-day business and forget the important tasks relating to learning transfer.

Agree with the managers that this 'nudging' will happen. Remember that they may well find these nudges annoying if they are not fully bought into the idea that their job is to help and support the trainee.

109. Delegate goals

We all know how important it is to set goals to help us choose our direction of travel. For the trainees, it's no different; they must have goals, but not just any goals. Their goals for the learning programme must be aligned with those the programme sponsors want the learning programme to achieve. They need to dovetail into and support the primary programme outcomes.

This seems obvious, yet how often do we find that trainees on a course have little or no clarity about the course outcomes? Without that clarity, how can they set themselves goals that will in turn support the programme goals? The programme goals must be explicit, understandable and something that managers and their trainees can buy into. They need to have these higher-level goals before the programme starts so they can discuss them and build them into how they will manage learning transfer. These goals may well have come out of the initial performance diagnostics process, but it makes good sense to revisit them with the project sponsor and ensure you have a set of evidence criteria they are happy with.

For the trainees, what are their personal success criteria? What do they see as the gap they need to cross to succeed? How will they know they have crossed the gap?

Story: Personal Learning Journal
Contributed by: Harry Bundred
Director of The Institute of Training & Occupational
Learning (ITOL)

ITOL published a small reflective learning journal to help people reflect on their experiences. With special thanks to Harry Bundred and ITOL, here is the text:

"It is not sufficient simply to have an experience in order to learn. Without reflecting upon this experience, it may quickly be forgotten, or its learning potential lost. It is from the feelings and thoughts emerging from this reflection that generalisations or concepts can be generated. And it is generalisations that allow new situations to be tackled effectively."

Personal Learning Journals can be a very valuable part of the professional development process. The key is to have a focus and purpose, and also to have a clear approach to the kind of critical thinking necessary to make it a fruitful experience.

Any Harry Potter fans may remember a conversation between Harry and Dumbledore about the 'pensieve'. In *Harry Potter and the Goblet of Fire*, Dumbledore explains to the young Harry that the stone basin he calls the 'pensieve' is used to hold excess thoughts from one's mind so that they can be examined at leisure. "It becomes easier to spot patterns and links, you understand, when they are in this form", says Dumbledore.

It's a great analogy. OK, the 'pensieve' itself remains a figment of the imagination but the principle of 'downloading' – in our case into a journal – for the purpose of later examination is a sound one.

Here are some helpful terms:

Learning Experience: A learning experience can either be a dedicated course of training or it may be something in everyday life. Externalising your thoughts and observations as a physical record helps to ensure that your memory does not distort events over time and prevents you falling into the trap of taking what you have learned for granted.

Learning Journal: The journal or diary is the physical output of your personal reflections. One of the purposes of your journal is for you to easily find your entries and cross reference them with other entries so that you can develop strands of observation and gain new understanding.

Learning Event: A learning event is a moment in time, in which you believe that you have realised something new, gained some insight or maybe experienced a change in your understanding of something. Reflecting on the learning event could reveal insights that will further your personal and professional development.

Reflection Point: A Reflection point captures and records the main essence of the learning event; it will typically capture not only the facts but also your emotional response and the learning outcome. A fuller picture is produced if both subjective and objective perspectives are recorded.

Reflection Strand: It may be helpful to consider your journal entries as strands of observation that you will interweave with other strands coming from other learning events. When woven together the strands will eventually reveal patterns that may have otherwise been hidden and these will give you further insight and understanding.

Post Reflection: After the initial reflection it is beneficial to revisit the reflection point at a later time and ponder on your contemplation. During post reflection consider any changes to your perspective on the learning event; maybe you would now feel and behave differently.

What do we mean by 'reflection'?
Reflection is about thinking deeply about something so that you are able to understand it more thoroughly. It might include one or all of the following:
- Taking a 'step away' from ourselves to gain perspective.
- Reviewing or replaying an action or interaction to make sure nothing has been overlooked.
- Being brutally honest with yourself about your part in something.
- Evaluating everything available about an experience.
- Trying to find a clear way through something complicated to arrive at a conclusion.
- Finding connections and relationships, often between something abstract (such as a theory) and something concrete (such as an incident that occurred when working in a practical environment).

Ultimately, 'reflection' is about 'making sense of experience'.

Think of it as a cyclic process:
1. What happened? Give a description.
2. What are/were your feelings and emotional responses?
3. What was good? Bad?
4. What sense can you make of the situation?
5. What can you conclude generally from the experience?
6. What can you conclude specifically from your individual response?
7. What will you do differently in the future?
8. What is your plan of action now?

Cycle back to step one.

Reflection is not about describing an event in simply narrative terms. It's about capturing thoughts, understandings and critical insights.

Here is a pro-forma journal entry. Use it as it is or use it as a starting point to design your own. Remember the structure is nowhere near as important as the activity itself!

Journal Entry
- Name and date of event
- What I enjoyed about this event was:
- What I found difficult about this event was:
- What I found challenging about this event was:
- What I have learned is:
- What I have learned connects with:
- Ways in which I could apply what I have learned in this event:
- People I should talk to about what I have learned in this event:
- Other ways in which I intend to follow up are:
- Use this space for any additional thoughts, feelings or connections you haven't noted elsewhere:

© Institute of Training & Occupational Learning 2013
Contact: itol@learning-transfer-at-work.com

110. What is the 'golden thread'?

The golden thread links your day-to-day actions to the vision and purpose of your organisation. If an organisation is clear on what it is and why it exists, the golden thread is bright and visible to all. And everyone goes about their daily tasks with a sense of purpose.

There is an apocryphal story about President John F Kennedy. When he was visiting the NASA space centre in 1962, he noticed a janitor and interrupted his tour to ask, "Hi, I'm Jack Kennedy. What are you doing?" The janitor responded, "Well, Mr President, I'm helping put a man on the moon".

The golden thread you need to pay attention to is the one that connects the programme you are designing with the wider organisational strategy and mission. How can you articulate this to stakeholders? How is your learning/performance programme going to ensure the larger strategy can be executed? Give people a clear line of sight along that golden thread or you will struggle to gain their support.

111. Do the trainees know what their job is?

This may seem like an odd question, but in today's fast-moving and high-change world, many trainees will either be in the midst of change in their job roles and responsibilities or in temporary positions. This uncertainty can cause them to sit back and wait for clarity before trying to use anything new they have learned on a training course. This, of course, speaks to the need for the training material to be directly relevant to the needs of the trainees, and for them to be able to see that need, and understand how it can tangibly improve their job performance. This in turn highlights the fact that the trainer needs to understand the work context of the trainee in enough detail to help link the training material to real-life workflow situations.

112. Risk management

When trainees try out new things after a training course, there is risk. Your design must cater for and manage this risk. The reason for this is that if the trainee and their manager do not see that the reward outweighs the risk, they will not undertake your carefully-designed learning transfer activities. Therefore, you need clarity on what sort of risk your activities involve, the appetite for risk within the culture generally, and specifically within the target audience. If they are very risk averse, you will need to set in place controls and processes to manage the risk appropriately.

The most obvious form of risk is people making mistakes when trying out something new, but there are also less obvious forms of risk. For example, what is the risk to ongoing operations if someone is 'distracted' with learning transfer activities? Without appropriate risk management, follow-up activities will not be done, and the whole learning transfer process comes crashing down.

113. What is the training for?

It seems crazy that I even have to write this, but I've asked this question of L&D practitioners in the past, and they have been unable to give me a straight answer. They weren't sure because they were on autopilot - doing what they have always done.

What is the training for?
- Behaviour change?
- Onboarding?
- Just in case, for bench strength?
- Qualifications required for operational licenses?
- Emergency response knowledge?
- Pure staff benefit and no direct work transfer?
- Whim of a very senior manager?
- Morale?
- Tradition? :-)
- Something else?

114. Flip your classroom

Flipped learning is a pedagogical approach in which the conventional notion of classroom-based learning is inverted. Students are introduced to the learning material before class, with classroom time then being used to deepen understanding through discussion with peers and problem-solving activities facilitated by teachers. The dramatic growth of online content creation, collaboration and distribution tools has provided an accessible toolkit for delivering flipped classroom learning.

Have you ever sat through a punishing training event where the trainer droned on while cycling through hundreds of PowerPoint slides? This 'jug and mug' approach to training is still far too common. It never really worked for traditional learning and works even less well when used as the starting point for learning transfer. As far as you can, take anything related to knowledge acquisition and transform it into self-study. Then spend your time in the classroom, after a quick content review, practising activities, applying concepts and ideas to problem scenarios, and interacting with peers and the facilitator. Also consider introducing some of the managers to this interactive classroom setting so they can introduce their practical experience into the mix.

A flipped classroom approach tends to set people up better for learning transfer than a traditional classroom approach. This is because in a flipped classroom it is all about doing, discussing, thought experiments, and finding ways to use the information. People get weaned off the idea that they go to the classroom to absorb new information. Don't call the self-study 'pre-workshop' or follow on activities as 'post-workshop'. Get away from the idea that the training workshop is the pivotal point around which other parts of the programme orbit. Treat it as a programme in which all components have value, and all components are necessary for a successful result.

Notice that the flipped classroom approach requires facilitation rather than a traditional training approach from whoever is leading the room. This can be a tough task for some trainers and they may need support to improve their facilitation skills. It also requires an acceptance by the trainees that things will be done differently on this training programme. It can be just as much of a shift for trainees used to traditional training as for the other stakeholders.

Story: Supporting Learning Transfer: Classroom to Workflow
Contributed by: Robb Sayers
Capability Lead, ViiV Healthcare and former Global Learning Consultant, GSK

Having been involved in training, people development & capability roles for almost 10 years, I have been through an endless array of feelings, frustrations and epiphanies when it comes to questioning why learning does not always 'stick' or, in our language, 'beat the forgetting curve'.

Essentially, in my early days as a trainer, I don't mind admitting that a job well done was when 'learners' left the classroom with a spring in their step and we were happy to review the positive happy sheets they left behind. It's not until I challenged myself harder that I began to question this as being just the start, the means to an end and the short-sighted (myopic even) route to performance improvement. After-all, training cannot be the only answer to fixing the problem. So how must the learning 'event' be woven in to a more meaningful experience, likely attached to project work, a challenging task or a higher rung than the perceived 'novice' status of our participants? Why wouldn't they just feel like receivers of training? I always remind myself that learning can happen without training and training can happen without learning. Fundamentally, they are not the same thing and helping learners recognise that they are the master of their own learning/development creates the correct accountability and commitment for new skills, knowledge or behaviours to be acquired and then applied for the benefit of their performance.

I have found that targeting learners when they are most primed to learning, that is to say when they are more open-eyed to the challenges that they face in their real world and the context in which they want and need to apply the learning, is most critical. In other words, do we always have the right learners in the room at the right time to receive the new knowledge, skills or behaviours that we assume they require, or perhaps their manager tells them? My most vivid example of this is when running project management training, hearing from five out the 10 learners that they are not currently managing any projects! I am not kidding, but it does beg the question: why were they there?!! I have never found a magic wand but more a checklist of different tactics, tips & tricks that have made the biggest difference to learning transfer in my experience.

- Involve the learner in the design of their experience. What will need to happen before, during and after to ensure the experience yields the results **they** want?
- Involve the manager. Share what was learned in the classroom and be explicit with the role they play. I have shared learning logs, text messages and video blogs to engage managers and create ownership for them to take the hand of the learner, show an interest in what has been learned and what support is required moving forwards.
- During the learning event, have self-formed study groups consolidate their learning and action steps and

share with the wider group.

- Further to the previous point, create accountability groups or buddies to continue the discussion on follow-up teleconferences, Skype or webinars.
- Frame questions such as: What will you be doing differently tomorrow, seeing differently in one week, and feeling differently in one month?
- Barrier busting. Have the group list out all the obstacles to them not implementing what they have learned. Prioritise the top three and create an action plan to build a strategy to overcome them.
- Alumni. Connect learners with a wider pool of like-minded individuals who can coach and support others in similar challenges or where experience can benefit others.

In short, I don't think I have cracked the answer to how you can ensure learning transfer each and every time, more just how can you challenge yourself and the student to consider the 'event' as part of a bigger commitment to performance improvement. I have always found that the three Ls hold me in best stead when diagnosing and designing optimised learning experience(s):

L1 (Learners): Who are the audience, what are their characteristics, challenges, styles, how many different audience groups am I working with?

L2 (Learning): Based on L1, how might the learning needs differ across different target groups? What knowledge and experience do they bring and what do they need to know, understand, do?

L3 (Logistics): If L1 and L2 are well defined, logistics can simply become the roadmap of what learning intervention(s), modality, format and performance support is required.

© Robb Sayers, 2018
Contact: robb.sayers@learning-transfer-at-work.com

115. But they won't do self-study!

A common criticism of giving people material to study outside of a classroom setting is that they simply won't do it. This is certainly true if you give them a mass of material and simply tell them to read it when they have time. You cannot just throw it over the fence and expect them to do anything with it. Where classroom study has a problem with retention, self-study has a problem with compliance.

For self-study to be successful, it usually needs to be *directed* self-study. You need to manage the process, and this is another instance where the input of the local manager is critical.

If the managers were involved with the programme design, they know why the self-study is there and why it is an important and integral part of the whole programme.

How can you set things up so that managers hold the trainees accountable for all the components of the learning programme, including the self-study? How can you set up the activities so that they are interesting? One example is a self-score questionnaire that will help people learn about themselves. Another example is where the results must be brought to the classroom as part of a competition.

116. Have the trainees failed before the training?

Trainees who have already had an experience where they failed, though they might well have succeeded if they had done the training programme earlier, are more likely to respond to the relevance of the course that is obvious to them. Have them share their stories with those trainees who have not yet had a direct need for the programme content.

117. Facilitate, don't lecture

Which bits of a training course do you usually remember most easily? It is probably not the slick, logical presentation of information by the trainer. It is more often the interplay between trainees, the collaboration during exercises, and the scenarios presented by other trainees illustrating where they had problems and how they solved them. How many times have you heard the phrase "I learned as much from the other trainees as I learned from the trainer"?

Yes, as a trainer you need your platform skills, but you also need to facilitate sharing and discussion, and this can be difficult for someone who has become used to being the sage on the stage.

118. The workshop is a small piece of the programme

There must be a constant theme running through the training day that it is simply a small step in a larger journey to making a difference back in the workplace. The workshop is not a pivot point for the programme; it is just a point along the journey, and arguably, not even that important in many cases. I have seen training programmes where some employees missed the training event, and yet after six months you wouldn't have been able to tell from their performance relative to their colleagues which of them had attended the training.

119. Working together

Have the trainees work together in the event in ways that you want them to work together after the event. How will they need to work together after the course? How can you introduce this dynamic into the workshop: through discussions, collaborations, problem solving or thought experiments?

120. Get activities started

Trainees will engage in many follow-up activities. How can you get some of those activities started in the workshop so there is some momentum? Is there a way you can set up activities so they are ready to go as soon as the trainees go back to their workplace? Even better, how can you get them to initiate some of those activities before they attend the workshop?

121. Stability bias

Human memory is anything but stable: we constantly add knowledge to our memories as we learn, and lose access to knowledge as we forget. Yet people often make judgments and predictions about their memories that do not reflect this instability. The term *stability bias* refers to the human tendency to act as though one's memory will remain stable in the future. We are very poor judges of our capacity to remember.

What does this mean for learning transfer? One consequence of stability bias is that we often take poor-quality notes when the content being taught seems easy to understand. That feeling of ease seduces us into thinking we will 'obviously' remember it easily. How many times have you gone back to some notes and not had a clue what your few scribbled words mean? At the time you must have thought that your brief note was adequate.

Story: Phase 1 – Readiness
Contributed by: Rachel Puttick, Director – Like Learning Ltd

Readiness. For 20 plus years learning readiness has been a maddening question lingering in my mind. Are staff (of all shapes, sizes and seniority) ready to embark on a learning programme? What are the advantages and disadvantages of undertaking a learner readiness assessment? How do you go about reviewing individuals' readiness for a learning event or programme? (Note, I'm still looking for a suitable term for this, readiness assessment has a ring of school about it that I'd like to run away from). Whatever you wish to call it, this must be much more than the standard pre-training questionnaire.

Recently, following a communications course with delegates from an internationally renowned NGO, I knew that two thirds of the people leaving the room (an unusually high number, it was a small group) were going to initiate changes in their relationships at work and subsequently client feedback would improve, providing strong evidence for future project funding. For these participants, learning transfer is going to happen. Others, I was painfully aware, were simply not ready. For them, and their organisations, that training was a waste of three days and precious resources. This is just one example and the phenomena can apply to all sorts of topics and titles from new receptionists through to Director Generals.

Perhaps these types of participants have too many elephant-sized problems on their plate to deal with. It could be a question of courage. Perhaps the person is not yet psychologically ready to rise up to the behavioural challenges (theirs and others) that they need to change for the good of the organisation. Or, on a practical note, perhaps there are simply not enough hours in the day to consider how and when to implement and reflect on the learning. The tangible issues can be resolved by re-allocating or reprioritising work. The intangibles can be resolved by further personal development; coaching; and ensuring a learning culture – all easier said than done albeit vital to the development and success of the company.

If a delegate is not ready to learn and go through all phases of the learning programme, then Finance have every reason to see the learning programme as a cost and not an investment.

Whilst on the subject of costs versus investment, assessing organisational readiness is an essential undertaking and equally crucial to the success of the learning intervention.

Certainly, what a phase 1 learning readiness assessment looks like will depend on the make-up and culture of your organisation and specific challenges you face. I advocate reviewing readiness through self-assessment rather than a top down pass or fail approach.

The disadvantage of staff assessing their own learning readiness is that it may uncover further issues such as cultural barriers or lack of leadership that the initial performance review did not reveal. In the long run that is of course an advantage; in the short term it can feel overwhelming. Also, people may not have the level of self-awareness necessary to undertake the review at that stage. People who back away from training/learning at work may use the assessment as an excuse, and managers may need courageous conversations support to be able to deal with this kind of attitude.

The advantages of doing a readiness review as a self-assessment are that:

  a. You are treating the people about to embark on a learning programme as equal adults, able to determine their own learning readiness.
  b. You are focussing people's minds on to the fact that this is a learning programme consisting of several phases, not a day out to have a bit of fun training! Immediately you are managing the expectations of all those involved.
  c. You avoid the dangers inherent in management decisions standing alone; such as labelling theory whereby one individual has been deemed 'untrainable', or unconscious bias that leads to one individual being deemed 'ready' and another 'unready'.
  d. Where people are psychologically 'unready' you can further investigate this and deliver learning that brings people up to the levels of readiness you need to make the programme a success.

What would a readiness review look like?

Shorter is sweeter, covering a range of questions:

  1. What do you personally want to be able to do back in the work place following this course?
  2. How will you manage your diary to find time to reflect on how you have used the learning, following the course?
  3. When, and how, following the course will you be able to start using the learning?
  4. What may inhibit your ability to implement the learning you expect to get from this programme? Think about organisational and team factors, and your own personal circumstances.
  5. How does this training fit with the organisations' and your teams' strategic aims?

6. How would you assess your own reactions to instigating change within your team? Are you filled with fear or feeling charged up and ready to go?
7. What would best support you in implementing the learning you'll achieve on this programme? [Insert a range of options such as post learning cohorts; online scheduled peer discussions; external coaches; allocated learning time; according to what is possible in your organisation].

You may have less bums on seats following a readiness review but at least they'll be the right bums.

© Rachel Puttick, 2018
Contact: rachel.puttick@learning-transfer-at-work.com

122. Discuss re-entry

Discuss the challenges inherent in going back to a workplace where colleagues have not been attending the same workshop. How will their colleagues and boss react on their return? Discuss ways that the trainee can get support and buy in from their colleagues to help them with the follow-up activities.

A friend of mine uses a puzzle as an analogy: if the trainee returns from the event as a differently-shaped piece of the puzzle, is it their responsibility or that of the organization to ensure that the space is now the right shape?

Ensure trainees, and their managers, know what commitments have been made by senior people to support them during re-entry, especially in terms of time to experiment and practise.

123. Self-coaching and reflection

Central to experimenting and practising new skills is the skill to self-coach and reflect. This is not a skill that comes naturally to many people, and yet it is so central to learning and development that it is worth helping people master it. One way to present this skill is in the guise of an after-action review. Another option is to teach them about the learning stack from Part 1 of this book.

Some call this a 'lesson learned' process but that sounds a bit punitive to the English ear; "He learnt his lesson!" Maybe call it insights or reflections or new wisdom, or actions to take forward.

124. Simulations and role play

Remove the need for trainees to imagine how they would use their skills when they return to work. Make it real for them by having the actual machine or tool in the classroom, or do role plays with each other or actors, or use computer simulations. Even just using videos of several different scenarios is better than relying on them to imagine what they will need to do from a description or diagram.

And then get them using their imagination to review and reflect on their experience of the simulations. Unless your simulations have been exhaustive in scope, trainees will always encounter different situations back at work, so you need to prepare them for those differences. What else could happen and what are the pointers that a situation is diverging from the one that has been practised?

Review the section on near and far transfer earlier in the book.

125. Making learning sticky

Roger Greenaway[13] has the following advice: "If near transfer is about making learning stick, then far transfer is about making learning sticky – keeping the original learning available for reuse in creative ways. Below are some lateral thinking tasks and questions that may help learners extend the value and application of their new learning".

- Recognise its value. List three reasons why this learning is important

---

13 *"Train the Trainer"*, Fenman (Issue 33, 2005) *Training for Transfer* by Roger Greenaway.

for you or for others.
- Imagine other possibilities. List three ways in which the learning could be used, if adapted.
- Find, create and use support. List three people who would readily support you in your efforts to use this learning in new ways.
- Prepare the ground. List three factors within your control that would make you more likely to use this learning in new ways.
- What if you could use this learning only three times before it expires? Which three situations would you choose?
- What if you could wave a magic wand and pass your learning on to everyone else in your team or organisation? What would be the result for you and the organisation?

In the same article he offers the following questions you could ask of trainees at the training event:
- What changes do you think will happen as a result of this training?
- How do you want to build on your existing strengths, skills and motivations?
- As a result of this training, what new ideas, skills or choices do you have?
- What new skills do you need to practise before using them for real?
- What do you want, or need, to try doing differently at work?
- What do you need to unlearn, to clear the way for the change you want?
- In what ways do you expect to benefit from what you have learned?
- In what ways might others benefit from the changes you want to make?
- What would be a highly successful outcome for your organisation?
- What will help you further improve your work performance?
- How will you continue learning and developing at work?

Dr Greenaway has published a lot of his research and thinking at http://reviewing.co.uk and I would recommend that you visit his site.

126. It's usually more than just doing

Successful transfer will normally require further learning and creative thinking, particularly if it is far transfer. It's important that trainees understand that there is more to do than simply apply what they have already learnt. When talking about the activities they will need to practise after the training event, make sure they realise these are still developmental opportunities.

127. The power of the debrief

There is a simple, powerful, yet underused tool for stimulating and reinforcing learning: debriefs. During a debrief, a team (or individual) reflects on a recent experience and identifies what went well and where improvement is possible. Debriefs can be conducted during training (for example, after a simulation or exercise), but they can also be a valuable tool in the post-training work environment, in which the focus is on work experiences that require the use of competencies acquired during training.

Debriefs provide an opportunity to self-correct and to reinforce what is working. When conducted after training, they can help uncover obstacles to transfer and lead to the establishment of goals or agreements about what to do going forward, which can help improve subsequent performance.

128. Prime directive of a manager

Peter Drucker once noted, "The productivity of work is not the responsibility of the worker but that of the manager". If you are a manager, you may be tempted to reply, "They don't have the skills they need", or "They don't care if the job gets done", or "The admin people keep causing them problems", or "The company doesn't give them the right tools", or even "But they are lazy!" These excuses cover up the fact that ALL these things are a manager's responsibility.

I have asked this question of hundreds of managers: "What do managers do?" I get a wide range of answers, but very seldom the one answer I hope for, which is "A manager's job is to help the people on their team be the best they can be and do the best job they can do".

To me, this is the prime directive of a manager and all their other management activities should be delivered through this as a filter. If all managers did this, what a difference it would make in general, and especially in learning transfer. It nurtures ideas such as

- Management is something you do 'for' people, not 'to' people
- Management is a service
- Management consists of getting the best out of people
- Management is more about others than about self.

Good managers manage performance, but great managers enable performance. When you are talking with managers about the operational effectiveness of people on their team, ask them this question and try and steer them into accepting/using this prime directive.

Story: Supporting line managers to play their part
Contributed by: Rachel Burnham at Burnham L&D Ltd

I think the very first thing is to be clear about is just how important the role of line managers is – share that fact with the line managers and with the key stakeholders for the programme. I think that sometimes we in L&D do ourselves no favours by acting as though we think that learning, and the full impact on performance in the workplace, can be achieved just through employees participating in a learning programme. And it can't.

Secondly, we need to invest in the skills managers need to support learning in the workplace – the key areas for me are providing regular and frequent feedback to team members, how to use work allocation to support the development of team members, and coaching skills.

Thirdly, I think it is worth thinking through, as part of the design of the programme, how to engage managers in the necessary support for learning transfer. There are many ways that this can be tackled, for example:
- Managers might participate in the programme themselves, perhaps ahead of their team members, so that they themselves can develop the skills and know

what 'good' looks like. Managers might even be used to cascade the learning and deliver it to team members.

- Managers could be invited to sample some of the programme, perhaps accompanied by a briefing session, so that they are clear about what good looks like after learning transfer and what the expectations are of how they can support their team members in developing their skills. There might even be an opportunity to practice observing and providing feedback to a team member or to practice encouraging reflection by a team member on their application of their learning.
- Managers could be briefed on the programme as part of a regular team meeting, again to establish what the expectations are of them in supporting this transfer of learning.
- Managers could be briefed through a webinar, video briefing or written briefing that they can access in their own time and review as and when they need it.

Fourthly, if we want managers to play a full part in supporting the transfer of learning, we also need to hold them accountable for this. Accountability needs to be built into whatever reporting and review process is used in the organisation.

© Rachel Burnham, 2018
Contact: rachel.burnham@learning-transfer-at-work.com

129. Fit to be a manager?

In an article published by *Harvard Business Review* (January 23, 2014), Monique Valcour ups the ante and claims that "If you as a manager are not helping people develop, then you are really not management material". This makes perfect sense if you believe that most learning and development happens on the job through new challenges and development opportunities in real-life projects, rather than mainly through formal training.

130. Managers see a bigger picture

Employees often miss the big picture of their company's mid- and long-term goals. Managers, on the other hand, have a higher-level view, and usually a better understanding of the company. Because of this, an important aspect of a manager's role in training is to help trainees see how their training fits into the company's overall plan. Managers should explain to employees the end goal of their training, let them know what kind of development should be prioritized (and why), and guide them on how to leverage their new skills to advance their role.

131. Beware of conventional wisdom

Conventional wisdom refers to the commonly-held beliefs, ideas and assumptions that a community or population has about an issue. These lead to a set of expectations, interpretations and explanations that people assume are true. As a result, the ideas embedded in conventional wisdom are rarely challenged. Even if people acknowledge there is a better way to do something, conventional wisdom may still rule the day.

Conventional wisdom has its value, but it can get in the way of change. On their return to the workplace, learners with fledgling knowledge and skills will encounter more experienced colleagues or managers who may, either consciously or unconsciously, undo the newly-created learning by promoting the existing norms and ways of the community.

If the new behaviours from your training programme contravene conventional wisdom, how can you inoculate your learners against this conventional wisdom, so that it does not re-infect them when they return to the workplace? How can you support them to undertake what may be seen as maverick behaviours? And how can you encourage a new convention?

132. Insights for the manager

A manager who works with their employee as they go through training gains essential insight into the employee's character, skills, work ethic and agility. These insights remain useful long after the training programme has been completed.

Story: Top five wastes of money in management development programmes – or what not to do!
Contributed by: Rachel Lewis, Associate Professor at Kingston Business School.

1. Don't consider running a one-off training course

Management development needs to be long term (3 months plus) using a range of different methodologies (such as coaching, feedback and workshops). Note, it is not just about more is better, but about considering how each element of the programme addresses an objective or a particular competency/ type of behaviour. If you run a programme that uses both coaching and workshops – but both largely have the same content (i.e. only the delivery method is different), you will also be wasting your money.

2. Don't let your programme be a 'drop in the ocean'

Any training course that is delivered in isolation is set up to fail. To make sure you get the most out of your development programme, link it to current organisational initiatives and strategies, to other development programmes, to organisational values, to performance management programmes and selection systems. Think about how you can create the strongest network of links to other initiatives for your programme. The more it is networked and embedded into the organisational life of the manager, the more likely it is to have an impact on that manager.

3. Think about the process NOT the content

Many organisations will spend the bulk of their time choosing the right provider and right course – and therefore focusing on the intervention part of the programme. Instead, think of the development programme as three equally important phases:

- The pre-stage. This is the stage where you embed the programme within the organisation, develop objectives, secure buy-in and engagement.
- The intervention stage. This is the stage where you run the development activities themselves.
- The post-stage. We develop and sustain skills by both practice and feedback. After the intervention, therefore, managers need to be given opportunities to use their skills, given feedback on their skill development and provided support to continue to build and develop.

4. Don't attempt to run a programme without buy-in

Making sure all stakeholders in the process are on-board and supportive of the programme is vital to its ongoing success in sustaining change in managers. The key stakeholders you need buy-in from are:

Senior managers. Consider not just how to get them bought in to the programme, but also make sure that they are leading by example and displaying the behaviours you want your leaders throughout the organisation to display.

The managers themselves. Ensure that the managers feel confident in their skills, are engaged and see this programme as valuable opportunity for development. Avoid mandatory attendance – if you need to force managers to come, you are doing something wrong.

Direct reports. If direct reports are not prepared to be managed by their manager, the manager's skills are irrelevant. Therefore, involve direct reports in the development of the manager and the overall process to ensure reciprocity of skill development.

5. If the organisational doesn't reflect the programme aims, don't bother

Developing managers to be, for instance, participative people managers in an organisation that rewards and recognises outputs and tasks, or to be authentic and transparent in a highly guarded and hierarchical organisation, is unsustainable and therefore a waste of time. Managers will develop to be a reflection of the organisational culture. The best organisational culture in which management skills can thrive and develop is where there is open dialogue across all levels of the organisation and where respect and recognition for all employees is embedded and visible.

© Rachel Lewis, 2018
Contact: rachel.lewis@learning-transfer-at-work.com

Note: Dr Rachel Lewis and her company have worked with the CIPD on some research which culminated on the development of a set of practical tools and checklists that will help with learning transfer, especially when training managers.

https://www.cipd.co.uk/knowledge/culture/well-being/
developing-managers-report

133. Have the outcomes changed?

The programme should have clear outcomes that are maintained over time, and that clarity should cascade to everyone else involved. At different times during the programme, ask your stakeholders to play back to you what they think the programme outcome is. Have any of the goalposts changed?

134. Harvesting trainee experience

The trainees will go forth after the training and have experiences. They will learn things that are valuable to themselves, and potentially to other trainees, who are having slightly different experiences as they do their training follow-up activities. How can you harvest the richness that is available across all these trainee experiences? How can you then make the harvest available to the other trainees who can make best use of it?

The answer these days, particularly if you have geographic spread and need to scale, is a technology-based discussion/forum application, where people are encouraged to post their experiences, their discoveries and their realisations. This sharing is often such a key part of development and change that you probably need to find some way of making it mandatory. How can you set up activities after the training course that ensure that people are 'experimenting out loud'?

Story: Experiential learning and learning assumptions
Contributed by: Bryony Portsmouth
Researcher Developer at the University of Sheffield

Thursday 30th November at 3.30pm was 'ThirTEA', the university's annual call to take 30 extra minutes to consider or engage in development. I decided that, for my 30 minutes, I was going to build a model Buckyball (a hollow spherical molecule made up of carbon atoms linked in the same pattern of hexagons and pentagons you see on a soccer ball) using a specially designed kit. I have encouraged others to make these as part of an annual researcher showcase but I had never tried it myself.

The next 30 minutes turned out to be incredibly illuminating from a learning point of view, for so many reasons. Firstly, you need to know that I did not complete the Buckyball, so from the point of view of my original objective for the 30 minutes – mission not accomplished.

I didn't feel crushed or despondent, just baffled – I knew I should be able to do it. My colleagues had different responses to my lack of completion, some wanting to have a go to see if they could make it work, others offering encouragement, others reflecting back to me their own experiences of learning and the techniques they use.
- Here's how the process went:

- I started building without using any instructions
- When my progress slowed, I used 'here's one someone made earlier' (at the researcher showcase) as a visual reference point
- I got stuck
- I did a little bit of mistake repeating while I figured out another strategy
- I knew where the instructions were to be found but I momentarily though it'd be 'cheating' to look them up
- I knew I had the capability to achieve the build and felt something was amiss with the kit
- I counted the number of pentagons in the completed kit and the amount I had – they were different
- I looked up the instructions
- I compared them to the physical reference I had used
- I noticed the colour use for the completed one and the one in the instructions was different
- It was now obvious why I had lots of red pieces left over and not enough white pieces

Throughout, I made decisions based on unconscious assumptions, born of experience. Some of those assumptions were helpful and some were a hindrance – what category would you put each of the below in? Were there other assumptions that I made?
- I assumed it could be done
- I assumed the visual template was accurate
- I assumed prior knowledge would help me
- I assumed I had done it wrong
- I assumed I could do it without assistance
- I assumed repetition would resolve it
- I assumed using instructions was 'cheating'
- I assumed taking a break would enable a breakthrough
- I assumed there was an issue with the kit
- I assumed I would succeed

The main thing I was reminded of from this experience is that in learning, there is no getting it 'wrong'. All our experiences are useful, if we only take the time to reflect on them.

I also experienced the 'easy when you know how' effect – it took ten minutes to complete the Buckyball after I had read the instructions!

© Bryony Portsmouth, 2018
Contact: bryony.portsmouth@learning-transfer-at-work.com

135. Reminding people to change doesn't work

You can set up a portal and even send regular links to video clips and other content, but reminding people to change or shoving extra content at them seldom works. It just becomes nagging. Does nagging work when you want someone to change? Support and encouragement is usually needed, not just a prod from a digital system.

136. What will colleagues say?

What reception will the trainees get from their colleagues when they return to their job after the training event? In one study I read a trainee commented to the researchers, "When we come from our classes, many of our colleagues tease us about going to school… These remarks hurt us a bit… I don't want to show off what I've learned in front of them because they will tease me even more".

137. Conversation prompts

L&D can offer resources, training, and support to help managers effectively coach their teams. For example, conversation prompts can guide these types of check-in. Ask open-ended questions, such as "How have you applied what you've learned so far?" or "Is there an upcoming project where you can try out something you've learned recently?" These help prompt and connect the link between learning and performance.

138. Questions for reflection

People often value speed and agility and focusing on the future rather than looking backwards.

This ignores the fact that one of the most useful tools for learning transfer is reflection. There are four useful questions:
1. What did we set out to do?
2. What actually happened?
3. Why did it happen?
4. What will we do next time?

When applying learning, we need to acknowledge that we will make mistakes, and that we will need time to understand those mistakes and figure out changes we must make to avoid making those mistakes again. How can you ensure that trainees have the time to reflect, and that reflection takes place?

Charles Jennings, in his article 'The Power of Reflection in an Ever-Changing World', says "A good starting point for embedding reflection into daily work-flow is to approach the practice at two levels; individual reflection, and then reflection with colleagues and team members. Reflective practice itself doesn't 'just happen'. It is a learned process. It requires some degree of self-awareness and the ability to critically evaluate experiences, actions and results".

139. Stop trainees burning up on re-entry

Re-entry to work can be tough if no one has been handling your workload while you were away. Jobs have stacked up and there's a pile of emails that need attention. In that climate, the new ideas and information from the course become a rapidly-fading memory before you can even begin to think about using them.

Ideally, the managers work with the trainees before the course to plan how to handle the workload and how to manage re-entry. From the team's perspective, this needs to be positioned as genuine help for a colleague rather than an imposition on those team members who are not attending the course. It is also useful for trainees who attended the same course to team up as buddies to support each other through the re-entry period and beyond.

140. Keeping trainees focused

Once you have focused trainees on the need for learning transfer, you need to keep them focused. Ideally, the activities involved in learning transfer become part of their job, rather than an adjunct or extra to their job. Transferring the training room learning to effective new behaviours on the job should be one of their deliverables, and they should receive support and management input for this deliverable just as much as for any other. The routines and procedures they have in place to keep them focused on their normal work deliverables should now include nudges and reminders to keep them focused on their learning transfer deliverables.

How can you make learning transfer just another aspect of the job?

Story: Setting expectations for a management development programme
Contributed by: Graham Watson,
Head of Talent, Performance & Development at the British Council

Author note: I am grateful to Graham Watson for sending in a document that is used in a global organisation to position a workshop on 'Managing and Developing People'. The document introduces the workshop to delegates, explains who it is for, what the learning outcomes are, and sets expectations. Below, I have extracted sections that are relevant to learning transfer, which, by the way, are the bulk of the document.

Note: The formatting was much nicer in the original :-)

Nominations
Nominations to attend this workshop should be supported and endorsed by the employee's line manager. Both the employee and the manager are responsible for:
  • Meeting in advance of the workshop to review the programme and learning outcomes and agree the

specific focal point, learning goals and specific actions for use and transfer on return to work.

- We recommend this discussion incorporates feedback based on the most recent performance evaluation and any feedback received from the manager, direct reports and/or other feedback providers.
- Participants and managers jointly agree and capture learning goals in the attached MDP Planner.
- A further meeting should be booked with your manager to take place as soon as possible (within 10 days) of completing the workshop. This is to ensure new skills and approaches can be applied, practiced, supported and transferred to the participant's role and workplace.

Expectations of you during the workshop

You are required to attend all three days of the workshop, participating and contributing openly, honestly and positively to build skills, confidence and effectiveness, through a range of interactive activities. These might include discussion groups, case studies, scenario observations, coaching / feedback exercises and small and large group discovery and problem-solving exercises. Whilst your facilitator(s) will build, deliver and adapt the learning processes to meet as many of the group's learning needs as possible, what you take away from the workshop will be a direct result of what you personally invest in the programme - before, during and after attending.

After your workshop, we expect you to...

- Provide feedback and complete post-workshop evaluations. We will also contact you after three months of attending to review the learning outcomes/gains you have achieved. These may be paper-based, electronic or by phone.
- Implement and refine your MDP personal action plan on return to work and ensure actions are integrated into your ongoing performance discussion and reviews.
- Participate in any virtual Action Learning Sets (Yammer), teleconferences or additional webinars where these have been agreed by workshop participants/ facilitators.

- Use the Learning Management System to top-up any ongoing learning needs. This system will be demonstrated to you during the workshops, as a useful suite of learning resources to support your ongoing learning/training needs, and those of your direct reports.

After your workshop, we expect your manager to…
- Provide ongoing support and coaching through regular one-on-one reviews, so your progress and achievements are monitored and recorded in your ongoing performance discussion and reviews.
- Engage in any follow-up learning evaluation activities to validate the learning, value and investment gains being achieved.

Pre-workshop activities (what you need to do before attending)
What you take away from this workshop is directly dependent on how much you engage and invest in it – before, during and after attending. To derive the maximum benefit, you should discuss your learning goals with your manager before attending, and again, once you get back to work.

It is essential you are prepared, focused and fully engaged during your workshop so you can take away the learning that is most relevant to you (knowledge, skills, tools, techniques etc.) so that you can plan to use and apply them when you return to work.

Actions:
1. Arrange a one on one discussion with your manager to discuss the reasons why you are attending and clarify what you need to learn from participating in this workshop.
2. Before meeting your manager, set aside 30 minutes for (uninterrupted) personal reflection to review the workshop programme and learning outcomes and consider the following questions:
   - What does good people management and development look like, for you?

- What challenges or difficulties are you experiencing as a manager?
- What are your team experiencing? What feedback are you getting from them?
- What do you need to pay more attention to? What are your specific learning goals?
- What support will you need before, during and after the workshop?

Note: There are no right or wrong answers to these questions. This is about internalising your thoughts and ideas about what you need and as a basis of two-way discussion with your manager.

3. Meet with your manager to discuss your learning goals with your manager, working together to refine and prioritise them. Useful questions for you and your manager to consider:
   - What elements of this workshop (look at the programme together) are the most important areas to support your PM&D role, activities and deliverables?
   - What PM&D activities do you need to improve, be better/do differently or change? Why?
   - What knowledge, skills or techniques could help you to do this? What's missing for you?
   - What feedback will support this? From yourself, your manger, team? Who else?
   - What will good/better look like after the workshop? How could you track and measure this?
   - What could stop you/get in the way of using your new learning when you return to work?
   - What support do you need from your manger, your team and others?

4. Use the MDP Planner (attached) and start to draft three to five learning goals you need to achieve using this worksheet.

5. Book a review meeting (now) to meet with your manager within 10 days of returning to work.

Post-workshop activities (what you need to do after your workshop)

Your facilitator(s) and participants will support you to reflect on your learning goals and build action plans you can start to implement when you return to work. Part of the coaching work on the final day will also focus on this. We ask you to do the following once you have attended your workshop.

Actions:

1. Complete your electronic workshop evaluation form within three days of attending (using the link we will send to you).

2. Book a one-on-one meeting with you manager to review:
   - The overall workshop and what you have learnt – in relation to your needs and goals.
   - What you intend to do with your team and specifically how you will use the key insights, knowledge and skills you have gained from being on the programme with your team.
   - Review and refine your action plan together, so you are jointly focused on how you will start to make improvements or changes and how you will go about doing that.
   - Agree how you will measure and monitor your progress, how you will manage obstacles/barriers and how you will know when you have succeeded.
   - Capture your learning and progression in your L&D Plan, in the Performance Management Systems (My Performance or Teacher's Portfolio).

3. Join the People Management & Development Yammer Group for ongoing support, asking questions, share ongoing resources/materials and checking your progress with other participants. This is optional (but highly encouraged) and will help your learning to stick, overcome common hurdles and keep momentum going.

Your manager's role (before and after your attendance)

A separate document (Line Manager's Activities & Support) is attached for your reference and so you know what we have requested. We will send this to your line manager at the same time we send you your joining instructions.

We strongly advise you and your manager to meet before and after attending this workshop, otherwise you may be at a significant disadvantaged in terms of being able to use, apply and transfer your learning to your work. Additionally, it will undermine the return on investment that the organisation and your manger is making in you.

Author note: A summary table of activities was included with the main highlights. The attached planner had the following prompts:

1. My Learning Goals
Where am I now? Where do I want to be?
Why am I attending this workshop? Why now?
What do I need to do better or differently?
What evidence/measures support my views?
How will I benefit from improving and changing?

2. How will I get there?
What do I need to do after attending?
What specific activities will I change/improve?
How will I use and apply learning back at work?
Who can help and support me?

3. How will I know I've got there?
What will be different in three months' time?
When will I use/practice my new skills?
How will I get feedback and from whom?
What might get in the way/derail me?
What can I do to keep my plans on track?

© Graham Watson, 2018
Contact: graham.watson@learning-transfer-at-work.com

141.   Make it safe to seek support

How safe is it to not know something in your organisation? How safe is it to fail? How safe is it to seek support from others?

Creating a safe environment, in which people feel that it is okay to show that they might be ignorant on a topic or incapable of doing a task, is vital for learning transfer and long-lasting behaviour change. A supportive environment helps learners to be less concerned about what other people think, and more focused on what they need to do to enhance their performance. This is particularly important for those learners who tend towards a fixed mindset according to Carol Dweck's model. Allow learners the time and space to build relationships with facilitators and with each other. Building relationships takes time but is essential to trust and safety.

Encourage learners to explore new ideas and ways of doing things by valuing curiosity and fostering diverging ways of thinking about the task, problem or opportunity. Help them step out of learned behaviours and current routines and take managed risks when trying new ways of doing things.

142.   Practice makes perfect

Many people would say that this is not true and that practising the same thing repeatedly just makes that way of doing it permanent, even if it is wrong. In this they are not giving our unconscious mind the credit it deserves. Whenever we do something, we have within our mind a sense of how we would like it to turn out, even if that outcome is somewhat fuzzy, implicit and largely out of conscious awareness. In effect, we have a target and our unconscious mind is set up to zero in on that target for us. As we practise something, there is a successive approximation affect: each iteration brings us a little closer to the target, even if we are not consciously reflecting on what we did or what we got.

This process of zeroing in on our goal speeds up when we get input from someone who has been through the same process themselves and is already practised at doing what we are seeking to do. Expert input can also help us avoid taking a shortcut that might at first seem a good idea, but would lead us down the wrong road. Here again, the manager can come to the rescue.

143. Sharing stories

We can learn from our own experiences, and we can also learn from others when they recount their experiences and stories. Don't condemn new learners to struggle through on their own without the ability to tap into the experiences of those who have gone before. Set up systems so that people can share their experiences. In effect, help them 'learn out loud'.

I have come across L&D people who have said that we cannot let trainees 'get the answers' from previous trainees because in some way they think the learning is not valid or pure and in any case this is akin to 'cheating'. I don't care how they get the answers, but I do care how they utilise those answers in practice and create their own stories.

144. After action reviews

An After Action Review (AAR) is a simple process used by a team to capture the lessons learned from past successes and failures, with the goal of improving future performance. It is an opportunity for a team to reflect on a project, activity, event or task so that they can do better the next time. It can also be employed during a project to learn while doing. AARs should be carried out with an open spirit and no intent to blame. The American Army used the phrase "leave your rank at the door" to optimize learning in this process. Some groups document the review results; others prefer to emphasize the no-blame culture by having no written record. AARs can be short, frequent group process checks, or more extended, in-depth explorations.

- Hold the AAR immediately whilst all the participants are still available, and their memories are fresh. Learning can then be applied right away, even on the next day.
- Create the right climate. The ideal climate for an AAR to be successful is one of openness and commitment to learning. Everyone should participate in an atmosphere free from the concept of seniority or rank. AARs are learning events rather than critiques. They certainly should not be treated as personal performance evaluation.

- Appoint a facilitator. The facilitator of an AAR is not there to 'have' answers, but to help the team to 'learn' answers. People must be drawn out, both for their own learning and the group's learning.
- Ask 'what was supposed to happen?' The facilitator should start by dividing the event into discrete activities, each of which had (or should have had) an identifiable objective and plan of action. The discussion begins with the first activity: 'What was supposed to happen?'
- Ask 'what actually happened?' This means the team must understand and agree facts about what happened. Remember, though, that the aim is to identify a problem not a culprit.
- Now compare the plan with reality. The real learning begins as the team of teams compares the plan to what happened in reality and determines 'Why were there differences?' and 'What did we learn?' Identify and discuss successes and shortfalls. Put in place action plans to sustain the successes and to improve upon the shortfalls.
- Record the key points. Recording the key elements of an AAR clarifies what happened and compares it to what was supposed to happen. It facilitates sharing of learning experiences within the team and provides the basis for a broader learning programme in the organisation.

145. Ready, fire, aim

Experimenting with new things involves risk and starting before you have all your ducks lined up. It reminds me of the 'ready-fire-aim' approach, first proposed by Tom Peters and Robert Waterman in their book *In Search of Excellence*. Sometimes you just have to start doing something rather than analyse everything first, and then aim your next shot based on the results you get from your first one.

146. Agree measures BEFORE the programme starts

Agree ahead of time with the primary stakeholders whether the measures you are proposing are acceptable to them. There is no point in measuring stuff and finding out later that senior stakeholders think your measurement process is flawed in some way. Where possible, also agree ahead of time how you will analyse and present this data and when you will do so. Consider if it's possible to have a dashboard approach, so stakeholders can see at a glance on a regular basis how each needle is moving.

147. Did it work?

Don't think of your measures as measuring the training event. If you do that, you are focusing on the wrong place. We should be measuring how well the organisation is using the training programme to get results. Think about this quote from Robert McNamara, "Measure what is important, don't make important what you can measure".

Story: Using assessments creatively to aid learning transfer
Contributed by: Rachel Burnham at Burnham L&D Ltd

If you need to build assessments into a learning programme, because it is part of a qualification, or for compliance purposes, or in order for learners to demonstrate their competence, or as part of the evaluation strategy, why not use these as part of your strategy to aid learning transfer?

I often hear L&D professionals groaning about assessment as not being a useful component of a programme and being something that just needs to be done! And, at the same time, I often hear of assessments being limited to knowledge checks; testing recall of information often in the form of multiple choice tests or quizzes. I think we are missing a trick – assessment of learning can take place in many, many different forms and many of these other approaches can be very useful for enabling learners to transfer their learning into work.

For example, when assessing skills, it makes sense to assess the development of those skills by getting the learner to demonstrate that skill through a practical assessment. Examples include baking a cake – if developing baking skills;

writing a report – if developing report-writing skills; analysing data – if developing data analysis skills; repairing an engine – if developing engine repair skills; responding to a customer complaint – if developing complaint handling skills . . . the list goes on. Often actual work examples can be used, e.g. with report writing, engine repairing, with the added step of a check by a suitably competent person prior to the output being used, which could be part of the assessment process. The closer the assessment task is to the actual work task, the more effective it will be for aiding learning transfer.

Certainly, when it comes to qualifications, my experience is that participants are well motivated to complete the assessments, because they are an integral part of achieving that qualification. If in addition, the assessment closely reflects tasks that they need to do as part of their role, so much the better. For example, as part of a qualification for L&D professionals, I have designed assessments that include creating a guide for line managers to do coaching – to demonstrate their understanding of coaching; carrying out and documenting a learning needs discussion with an individual employee; reviewing assessment data and writing a report to present this analysis – to demonstrate data analysis skills; and developing a plan for a blended learning programme.

The assessments are created so that, as far as possible, participants can work on examples from their own workplace. These tasks are things that L&D professionals are likely to have to do in their professional role, so completion of the assessments helps the learner develop confidence and also shows their colleagues what they are capable of. Both aid learning transfer.

So, one way we can improve at supporting learning transfer is to get better at designing useful assessments!

© Rachel Burnham, 2018
Contact: rachel.burnham@learning-transfer-at-work.com

148. Consider setting up control groups

If the scale of the programme is large enough, consider setting up control groups who have yet to go through the programme, so you can compare their performance with that of former trainees. You could do this at the macro level covering the entire programme, or split-test components of the programme to figure out which versions/options work best.

149. A better question about measurement

An L&D manager once said to me that they were measuring performance after a training course to answer the question "What impact did the training have?"

I pointed out that a better question after a training course is "Did the training have the impact it was designed to have?", because this question forces you to think about what you wanted before you started. In effect you have a simple flow chart that shows
1. What is the business goal?
2. What do people need to do?
3. What do people need to learn?
4. What training is required?
5. Did they do the training?
6. Did they learn what was needed?
7. Are they now doing what they need to do?
8. Was the business goal achieved?

150. Why are you measuring?

Think first, why are you measuring? Is it because
- You need to report results to someone else?
- You need feedback on what you are doing so you can improve it?
- You like details and numbers and it just feels like the right thing to do?
- You need in-process measures to know early that you are off course?
- You were told to?
- You want data to back up your intuition?
- You find measurements motivational for yourself and others?
- Other reasons?

For each of the reasons above, what will happen to the measures? What response will they generate? Too often measures are put in place and only after the figures come in do people say, "That's interesting; what should we do about it?" For each measure you put in place, figure out beforehand what you will do in response to the measure changing. If it changes by 10% we will do X; if it changes by 30%, we will do Y, and so on.

151. The fallacy of testing memorised information

Let's say you sit an exam at the end of the training event; the average score is 80% and most people are not far from that score. You might pat yourself on the back for that.

Let's say you do the same test six weeks later. What will the average score be if there has been no reinforcement of that memorised information? Maybe 20%?

Maybe the training should have only covered the 20% that was retained? If people are only going to be able to memorise and then recall 20% of the material, is it the best 20% from a business perspective? What if you sat the same exam again after three months?

What do you really want from the training programme and how can you measure that?

152. Data and intuition

We need both data and intuition. Malcolm Gladwell made a case for the amazing powers of intuition in his book *Blink* (April, 2007). For a more rigorous approach, with an extensive bibliography, get a copy of *Gut Feelings: The Intelligence of the Unconscious* (June, 2008) by Gerd Gigerenzer. Our intuition has been amazingly well honed over millennia to help us survive as a species. It is an awesome tool, and now we have data as well, which is just as awesome. Working together, data can turn a suspicion into a verifiable fact; it can trigger new intuitive thoughts seemingly unrelated to the original data, and intuition can help us decide what to measure when there is so much we could measure. We will always use intuition; it is our birthright and now, with the new data tools we have available, it has become more powerful than ever and serves as a partner for our intuition.

Consider this quote from Mark Twain, "It is not what we don't know that gets us into trouble. It is what we think we know for sure".

153. Presenting data

You have collected and analysed your data. Now you want to present it. Easy, you have Excel. Just knock up a couple of graphs and put them on a slide. Job done!

Your data will influence decisions to do something different or keep doing the same thing. Arguably, if it has no influence at all, why are you bothering to collect it? The way you present your data affects its credibility and decides which aspects of the data people focus on. You also want the discussion to move on from the data to the next decision - whether that is about tactical tweaks or larger-strategy shifts. Badly-presented data often gets people discussing the data rather than what they will do because of the data. Well-presented data can produce effective action and enhance your brand.

- Think first. What is the message you want the data to convey? How do you want people to feel after they see the data?
- Don't be sloppy. Your data presentation affects what people think of you, and therefore your brand.
- What are the minimum data you need to get the point across? The detail data may be important to you, but maybe the general trend indicated by the data is enough?
- How long does someone unfamiliar with the data need to look at your chart to figure out what it signifies? If you want the data to trigger actions, you need a fast and visceral response.
- Experiment with different views or ways of presenting the data and try them out on people. Figures or charts? Which kind of chart?
- Aggregate data and see if this loses any necessary detail.
- Have a simple chart and then an optional secondary one that includes extra details for the same data, such as data points and graduated axes.

Story: Tracking engagement with learning
Contributed by: Toby Newman, Global Trainer

We tracked hours of training completed that told us little and did not demonstrate that the learning was being applied. We have now pushed the responsibility for successfully applying learning to their role back to the individual – very much a trust thing! We are looking at tracking engagement as an indicator to see if a person is at least engaged in the learning programme. The thinking is – the more someone engages with learners and colleagues on a training topic, the more likely they are to be invested in improving themselves.

There are currently two main ways we are tracking engagement – we use Yammer as our main communications tool and we have set up a main training group that we track with regards to 'number of likes', and 'number of comments made'. We will also be setting up specific Yammer groups for dedicated training curriculums, so we can see how engaged people are on specific topics.

The other means is via survey. We have a regular Pulse Survey which asks questions such as if the person feels they are achieving their goals and do they feel their training needs have been met.

We are also currently increasing the training for managers so that they can 'track' their staff through Personal Development Plans.

© Toby Newman, 2018
Contact: toby.newman@learning-transfer-at-work.com

154.   Measure in the middle

Don't just think of measures as something that happens at the beginning for a benchmark and at the end to judge success. A full learning transfer programme will likely last a few months or even more than a year. You need to measure along the way, so you can make corrections. In process measures tell people how they are doing *now*. Smaller corrections now are easier than bigger corrections later. Knowing at the end whether you did well or not is interesting. Knowing *why* you did well or not is useful for next time.

155.   Measures versus metrics

There is an old saying: "What gets measured gets done." And there's the corollary, "If you can measure it, you can manage it." But be careful here. There is also another old saying: "Weighing a pig every day doesn't make it grow any faster".

You certainly need to measure, but you also need to relate those measures to other factors to turn them into a metric that can guide decision making. For example, changing the feed regime of the pig and relating this to the pig's weight changes gives you a valuable metric you can use to optimise weight gain.

Figure out what decisions you need to make, and then you can figure out what metrics you need to make those decisions better.

156.   Competition/gamification

Can measures be applied to a cohort or group and posted in comparison to other groups? This is where you could start to introduce a sense of desire to do learning transfer well in comparison to others. However, be careful. Not all competition between colleagues is good for the organisation. Keep it light-hearted, and low on consequence. It may be better to focus on individuals reaching goals that are independent of whether others are doing it, so you don't make it about winners and losers. We have seen enough of the bad effects of this with the forced stack and rank systems of performance appraisals.

157. What you measure gets their attention

If people know you are measuring something, their attention will go there, and their behaviour will change, based on what they suspect your targets are for that measure, whether you have targets or not. Think about what measures you are using that you will make public and consider how those public measures will tend to focus attention. Also think about what behaviours you want to encourage, and then what measures you could put in place to influence that behaviour.

158. What reporting goes to whom?

Of the various measures you put in place, who gets the results? For example, which results are made available to the trainees themselves? Maybe all of them if you are operating in the spirit of transparency.

159. Measure value add

Take a step back and consider how the training programme and the desired behaviour changes are adding value to the organisation. Value can be added in many ways, such as increased revenue, decreased time, mitigated risk or higher morale. What sort of value are you seeking and how can you measure it?

160. Not all measures are quantitative

Given we are talking about behaviour, some of your measures will be qualitative rather than quantitative. In other words, anecdotal. How can you gather this anecdotal evidence, and then how can you present it usefully to the programme stakeholders?

How can you avoid bias when evaluating anecdotal evidence? For example, just because a few trainees shout about something, this does not mean it is a common experience for all trainees.

What does the anecdotal evidence really tell us? Have a look at Robert O. Brinkerhoff's book *The Success Case Method* (January 2003) for a quick, practical, and accurate evaluation approach that provides credible information about the success of a change initiative: what results it is getting, what is working, what is not, and how it can be improved.

If you just look at the average results across the cohort, it will probably look as if the training course is not helping very much. The middle of the bell curve tells you less than the outliers. So, look at the people who have made the most of it. If there are none of these, then throw the course out the window. If there are a few of these, and particularly if they have done VERY well because of the programme, then you know the programme can work. Look for measures that will help you understand what the people who are succeeding with their learning transfer have done differently to those who are not doing so well.

161. Beware of aggregated data

In a world of 'big data' we often resort to using averages, aggregates and algorithms. While insightful sources of trend information, these nullify the idiosyncrasies of individuals. The process of aggregation can smooth out the data and make us lose sight of blips that may be important. Have a look at the raw data for outliers, just in case there is a blip that could be useful.

162. Do any of the measures threaten people?

Could any of the measures you are proposing be perceived as a threat? If there are targets, perceived or real, what happens if people do not reach that target? Are any of the measures likely to become an end in and of themselves? In other words, will people seek to meet the measure and lose sight of the primary performance outcomes?

163. Measures affect culture

What measures does the business already have in place? What do these say about the culture? If culture change is one of the required outputs, what new measures are needed or what changes could be made to existing measures to guide people's behaviour towards the new cultural requirements?

Existing measures may well be a barrier to the desired changes, as people routinely seek to meet the measures they are familiar with. If you are getting rid of a measure, be clear that it is gone. Have a public funeral for it.

164. Measure side effects

Are there any potential side effects of the training that are beneficial? For example, reduced absenteeism, reduced need to retrain if learning transfer is done well, less paperwork because there are fewer errors, less risk of employment tribunals and so on.

Story: Can you learn while you're asleep?
Contributed by: Stella Collins – Creative Director
Stellar Learning at www.stellarlearning.co.uk

Back in the 1960s there were optimistic experiments to determine whether people could learn languages or key facts whilst they were fast asleep. You'd go to sleep and experimenters played all kinds of fascinating resources to you and then, when you woke, you'd be tested to see what you've learned. Sadly, they found you can't really learn new information whilst being asleep. However, the latest evidence from neuroscience and sleep research reveals that sleep is vital for consolidating learning and that it's possible to do some minimal conditional learning associating sounds and smells, for instance.

Even the experts are still not sure why we sleep but the evidence is that, without sleep, we fail to learn. You're going to explore what happens in different sleep phases and some suggestions for you as learning practitioners, your learners and your organisations.

In certain phases of sleep your brain is as active as when you're awake as it works hard to store up and consolidate your memory of a day's learning. Sleep phases can be observed with electroencephalograms (EEG) to measure electrical activity emitted from your brain. When you're awake and consciously paying attention, your brain emits relatively high frequency beta waves. As you go through various stages of sleep these brain waves change. The relaxation you feel as you drift off, and also when you wake up in the morning, is characterised by lower frequency alpha brain waves. You also experience alpha waves when you're daydreaming or relaxing, physically and mentally. As you pass into deep sleep your dominant brain waves change to the slowest of all, delta waves. Later in the night, when you start to dream in what's called Rapid Eye Movement (REM) sleep, the patterns change to mainly theta waves.

Brain waves were named in order of discovery rather than frequency. Our fastest brain waves, gamma, were discovered last and are associated with insights, or literally having a 'brain wave'.

How does this relate to learning? When you're focused, beta brain waves dominate, and information is fed from your sensory systems to multiple places in your brain. Some of it arrives at the hippocampus to begin the complex process of long term memory formation. During the day high levels of the neurotransmitter acetyl choline seem to influence the direction of this information to your hippocampus.

When you day dream or relax, patterns of activity switch to slower frequency alpha waves. In this state your brain is often more active across its entirety rather than having a narrow focus, potentially enabling you to connect ideas, thoughts, sensations and leading to more creative thinking.

Research shows that, when we dream, we appear to rehearse patterns of behaviour, especially motor skills. If you were to learn a simple pattern of finger movements and get tested just before you went to sleep, you would find you'd improved during the learning period. However, the next morning you'll actually be even better at it, as long as a mean sleep researcher didn't wake you up and disturb your dream (REM) sleep; in which case you'll be no better than the night before - possibly even a little worse. Lower levels of night time noradrenaline (a stress hormone) may allow you to 'review' emotionally upsetting episodes with less emotion; perhaps a reason for the old formula 'time heals' – it's not actually the time but the sleep that does the healing.

Equally as important as dream sleep, is the *quality* and *quantity* of deep sleep you get. During these slow wave delta phases levels of acetyl choline drop significantly. It appears that lower acetyl choline levels allow the information that you've stored in your hippocampus to flow back out to the relevant storage areas for your new memories. Without deep sleep you can't form long term memories and therefore you can't learn.

So it doesn't matter how well designed your learning sessions are; if your participants don't get a good night of sleep afterwards, their ability to lay down memories is impaired.

Practical ideas to try
We may not have enormous control over the sleep patterns of our participants, so what can we do practically to harness the value of sleep rather than work against it?

First of all, we can educate ourselves about why sleep is so vital and then share that with our learners. Students or people learning for exams often cram information late at night, missing out on vital sleep that will strengthen their memories for the next day's test.

One of the biggest barriers to a good night sleep is the blue light emitted by electronic devices such as TVs or mobile phones. Blue light stimulates melatonin production, which regulates our sleep patterns. Higher levels of melatonin keep you awake, so checking your messages before bed is a sure fire way to disrupt your sleep. Perhaps, rather than ban the use of phones, we could encourage people to use them during the day and suggest they turn them off a couple of hours before bed, or at the very least switch them to 'night mode', which filters some of the blue light.

Similarly, rooms that are too warm prevent good sleep. A lower core body temperature is a signal for your brain to sleep so if, like me, you end up in a hot, stuffy hotel room, open the windows or give the aircon a blast of cold as you get ready for bed. A warm bath, somewhat counter intuitively, lowers your core temperature because it sends blood to your extremities.

What we learn and *when* we learn it, may be important. It may pay to do physical elements of learning later in the day so there's less information to interfere before people get a chance to rehearse it in their dreams. This is another good reason to link physical activity to cognitive learning.

A short nap has consistently been shown to improve performance, possibly because it increases the opportunity to consolidate memories. Though a short nap is unlikely to get you into deep delta wave sleep, it will allow alpha waves to dominate inspiring creative thinking and connection. After you've covered a number of concepts in the morning try a relaxation activity or guided visualisation after lunch and work with the body's natural rhythms.

Away days or workshops are increasingly being cut down from a few days to just one day. But if we really want people to benefit from the reduced formal learning, they are offered that it might be better to split sessions across two half days rather than one single day. That way you've got two nights of sleep to embed the same amount of information more firmly into memory.

Whatever you decide to do, you'll rarely regret getting more sleep.

© Stella Collins, 2018
Contact: stella.collins@learning-transfer-at-work.com

165. Celebrate success and share good news

When your trainees do something great because of being on your training programme, shout about it. Notice I said 'when' not 'if' :-)

Your training must work and be seen to work because that helps people who are still on the programme and are busy transferring their learning; it also helps future trainees.

166. A transfer exercise

Your mission now, should you decide to accept it (don't panic, this book won't self-destruct!) is to transfer what you have learned from the book to your work. It sounds simple, but how will you do it? Here are some ideas...

- Use a highlighter as suggested to mark up ideas that can help you
- Add some tasks to your to-do list RIGHT NOW
- Make a list of questions to discuss with colleagues
- Look at a current training programme and think of at least three ways to improve it
- Apply these ideas to a programme that is in development
- Read your L&D strategy, and maybe rethink it
- Contact me, the author, with feedback or questions.

Or will you just let the ideas float around in your mind for a while and hope they will re-emerge in some useful form when you need them? Remember ISLAGIATT!

If you want to make a difference, be proactive and transfer your own learning. I can't do it for you.

Companion Reading

Here are a few books I would highly recommend. Partly because they have shaped my thinking concerning learning transfer, but mostly because they incorporate practical tools and tips that will make your life easier as you transition to a learning transfer focused approach.

"What Makes Training Really Work: 12 Levers of Transfer Effectiveness"
Dr Ina Weinbauer-Heidel
ITE, 2016, ISBN (English edition) 9783746942995
The author presents a conclusive framework based on a solid scientific foundation, along with more than 50 tools and interventions that HR developers, training providers and trainers can use to maximise the effectiveness of any training course or programme. After reading this book, you won't be able to say, "I don't know what to do" with regards to learning transfer.

"Learning Paths: Increase Profits by Reducing the Time It Takes Employees to Get Up-To-Speed"
Jim Williams and Steve Rosenbaum
Pfeiffer/ASTD, 2004, ISBN: 9781118673720
The authors use a learning paths methodology to focus on reducing the time to proficiency and reduce classroom time. It is a detailed system with templates and tools that is ready to implement. The system will ensure you are doing the right training, and doing the training right. The book has a good blend of strategy and tactics. In the foreword, Ed Robbins says "If you are an HRD professional, it's like being a kid in a candy store".

"The Six Disciplines of Breakthrough Learning: How to Turn Training and Development into Business Results"
Calhoun Wick, Roy Pollock, Andrew Jefferson
Pfeiffer, 2010, ISBN: 9780470526521
Also by the same authors…

"The Field Guide to the 6Ds: How to Use the Six Disciplines to Transform Learning into Business Results"
Wiley, 2014, ISBN: 9781118648131
The six disciplines approach provides practical methods, tools, roadmaps, and checklists for bridging the 'learning-doing' gap. The 6Ds encompass the entire process of converting learning into improved performance, from pre-course communications to the impact of the learning transfer climate. The Field Guide adds even more case studies tools and guidelines from around the globe.

"Mindset: How You Can Fulfil Your Potential"
Carol Dweck
Robinson, 2006, then updated 2017, ISBN: 9781472139955
In the introduction, Carol Dweck says "In this book, you'll learn how a simple belief about yourself – a belief we discovered in our research – guides a large part of your life. In fact, it permeates every part of your life. Much of what you think of as your personality actually grows out of this 'mindset'. Much of what may be preventing you from fulfilling your potential grows out of it." Dweck's mindset model has immense implications for those wishing to help others improve and grow through learning and subsequent learning transfer.

About the author

Paul's life and work history can only be described as a little unusual.

He grew up on a hill country farm in New Zealand and went on to study both Agriculture and Engineering at University. He graduated with first class honours and a couple of years later won a national farm machinery award for the design of a seed drill. The drills were exported by his employer to over 20 countries around the world. Years later, when he was travelling in Ecuador, he was amazed to see one of his seed drills up for sale in a second-hand farm machinery yard by the side of the road.

As many Kiwis do, he set off to see the world and travelled extensively, stopping along the way to earn money for the next adventure. He then landed what was to him a dream job, working for an adventure travel company leading overland expeditions into many remote areas of the world. All this experience, which lasted over four years, has given him some great stories to tell of far-flung places, from the Congo jungle to the Taklamakan desert in Western China. By the way, locals say the name means 'go in and you will never come out'.

Paul then 'got a real job' as an engineer in the UK. It proved quite a challenge to make the transition from travelling the wild places on the planet and needing to build a campfire each night, to working regular hours and commuting.

After some success, he was headhunted into a NASDAQ-quoted multi-national technology company, where he eventually held the role of Customer Services Director. It was during this time that he really started to appreciate the impor- tance of learning, and was surprised that his adventures and the experience of observing people learn to cope with unfamiliar situations were so valuable in understanding learning. His curiosity led him into studying psychology and many other areas relating to how the mind works – knowledge which he could then translate back into the workplace.

The constraints of corporate life lost their appeal and Paul started his own company, People Alchemy Ltd, in 1999, working as a consultant, trainer and coach in the areas of management and leadership. Most of his clients were blue chip organisations and one client programme had over 1,200 delegates.

He soon started seeing gaps in the traditional approach to learning and development, and how those gaps were leading to results that were anathema to his engineering mind. He recognised the need for more direct performance support and the importance of informal learning in all its guises, rather than the common L&D reliance on classroom training which had its own problems due to lack of learning transfer.

Paul has a way of engaging people with this changing paradigm, so they can grasp it, incorporating it into their own organisational learning and capability strategies. He likes to say that he helps translate people's reality so they understand what they need to do next to make a difference. His approach enables people to fully cater to the learning needs of their staff, so they can get the job done.

INDEX

amount of information required in
programmes, 129
appeal of programme, 167-8
branding of programmes, 88
defining results measurement at
design stage, 83-4, 94
experience design, 130
involving managers, 127, 132
levers for effective learning
transfer, 71-3
minimising effort required by
trainees, 135-6
order of planning, 126
post-training activities, 161, 168-9
understanding work context, 162
training programmes
see also workshops
amount of information required, 129
as part of workflow, 188
branding, 88
celebrating success, 228
control groups, 217
debriefs, 195
effortless experiences, 135-6
engaging employees, 126-7
engaging managers, 127
goals, 177-8
joining instructions, 143
marketing, 166
measuring results, *see* results,
measurement
modification to include learning
transfer, 15-17
outcomes, 201
post-programme action plans, 163-5
post-programme behaviour, 93
predicting consequences, 85
requirement for, 25-6
responsibility for, 99
side effects, 224
success rate, 81
support for organisational
strategy, 181-2
value added to organisation by, 222
Training Zone, 8
transfer theory, 53

U

'understanding', 114
Unlocking Potential (Towards Maturity
benchmark report), 5

V

Valcour, Monique, 197
Viral Change, (Dr Leandro Herrero), 102
volition, 138-9
Vygotsky, Lev, 34

W

Waterman, Robert, 214
Weinbauer-Heidel, Dr Ina, 69-70, 76
*What Makes Training Really Work: 12
Levers of Transfer Effectiveness*,
70-76, 229
Wentworth, David, 80
workplace environment
see also cultural environment
changes in, 159
competence of, 26-7
creating supportive environment, 212
inclusion in training design, 55-6
stress reduction, 149
workshops
see also training programmes
computer simulation, 193
debriefs, 195
goal-setting at end of workshop, 176
post-course fora, 201-2
role play, 193

X

xAPI, 86